Secrets
to Becoming a
Master
Networker

**A Power System which Creates
Leverage and Duplication
to Increase Revenue**

Stacey O'Byrne

ISBN 978-0-9883438-0-1

Printed in the United States of America
Instantpublisher.com

Printed in the United States of America
CreativeSpace.com

Praise for "Secrets to Becoming A Master Networker"

"Stacey O'Byrne's ability to teach a different perspective on "prospecting and sales" has made a tremendous difference in my business sales since I came from a nursing background. Secrets to Becoming a Master Networker has bridged the gap between those two worlds for me.

Building relationships of mutual respect & benefit, and nurturing them from a place of service, are principles that are often foreign in today's complex society. Stacey has captured the spirit of being authentic, transparent, and congruent and teaches how its natural application will make any business flourish!"

— MaryBeth Holleger, Crystal Executive, Isagenix International

"By learning the tools from this book, I took my hobby to a career. I am thrilled with my confidence as a business owner and networker. Thank you Stacey for these valuable tools."

— MaryLou Hunter, HHP,CN

"Secrets to Becoming a Master Networker gave me a totally different point of view on what real networking is, and clarified what I thought it was. I am very social and easily meet and talk with people, but that is not enough! Professional networking requires some effort in changing attitudes, but with the tips and tricks of this book this can be immediately put into practice and with great results!"

— Shelly Cady, Sales Representative, Liberty Mutual Insurance

"Secrets of a Master Networker goes beyond the global concepts you find in most of the business/self help books in the marketplace. This book actually reveals proven action steps, if you are motivated enough to invest your time and energy in the process, to positively impact the bottom line of your business. You will unlock your own personal blueprint on how to leverage your relationships into an unlimited stream of business. Stacey O'Byrne gets it right. Authenticity is essential to achieve the results you desire. This is the only book on networking you will ever need."

— Lisa Guzzo, Productivity and Organizing Consultant

Praise for "Secrets to Becoming A Master Networker"

"Stacey O'Byrne will shift your networking paradigm! Secrets to Becoming a Master Networker is a value-packed, content-rich book that will change the way you think about and engage in your professional relationship building and networking activities. If you do, or plan on doing, any type of networking, Stacey challenges you to rethink, re-evaluate, and reform everything you thought you knew about the subject, and more importantly how to leverage your networking time and activity!

Stacey's business relationship management philosophy is highly evolved originating from her personal experience, inherent knowledge, and extensive research. Secrets to Becoming a Master Networker is hugely insightful and refreshing and has been incredibly valuable to me personally and professionally. Highly recommended!"

- Tim Watkins, Independent Associate, LegalShield, Inc.

"A must-have book for business owners and anyone interested in becoming successful in sales! Stacey's no-nonsense style makes this book a joy to read and the tools easy to apply instantly!"

- Marla Shaw, Marla Shaw Graphic Design

Dedication

ML, I can't thank you enough
for all you do for our family.
Peady Pot and Danni,
I love you with all my heart,
you make us so proud.
Mom and Tami,
your guidance, love and support
is the foundation to our lives.

Acknowledgements

*I wish to personally thank
the following people for their
contributions to my inspiration
and knowledge and other help
in creating this book: MaryLou,
Kiana, Danni, Mom, Tami, Marla,
Les, Cecile, Lisa, MaryBeth, Julie,
Erika, Kelli, Terilee, Tim, Sheldon,
Cory, Dawn, Eloise, and Karen.
You all ROCK!!! THANK YOU!!!*

Contents

Contents

Forward

Life is all about connections. There is something innate in the human animal that seeks out to be joined in concert with others. For thousands of years this basic compelling has driven mankind to create and destroy. The need to connect can inspire inventions such as the airplane, great architectural achievements such as the Roman Coliseum, or even intimate love sonnets. However, this primal instinct gone wrong can also lead the boycotting of airlines by unions, the overthrow of empires by coup d'états, and the harsh rejection of love spurned. What many fail to realize, and what Stacey O'Byrne has mastered, is that need to connect to others is the thing that can make or break any business.

If you've been in networking for a while, you know there are two types of people, acquaintances and partners. An acquaintance is the type of person you vaguely recognize when you see them. They are the one you sometimes travel the same circle as, and you refer to each other as "so-and-so" or "such-and-such." They know people - well, they know of people but have no close connections. And they are the ones that usually don't last long in business. They hit a crisis, a drop in sales, an immediate need for contacts, and they send out emails to a group list because they don't have phone numbers. They always bemoan that no one wants to help them get ahead. They are the ones that know things, but not people. Then there are partners. Partners are the people that know people, and the people they know are the people to know. Partners are what Stacey refers to as "centers of influence" because that is just what they weld, influence. When a partner hits a crisis, they can reach out to any number of people who will feel privileged to lend assistance. Partners know your name, remember where you met, what your specialty is, and think of how they can help you almost as much as they think of how you benefit them. They cultivate friendships for months just in the off chance you can one

Forward

day assist each other. And here's the thing, partners don't do this as part of some master manipulation, they authentically are committed to building relationships. Partners recognize that people want to be connected, and partners have the skill, means, and desire to be a hub of interpersonal connection.

Stacey O'Byrne is a proven Master Networker, and as I have witnessed firsthand, the very epitome of the "center of influence" she writes of in this book. Some people are born with this talent, and some (like me) develop it over time when faced with dire straits. Stacey falls into both of these categories. Blessed with a natural ability to lead, she discovered the secrets to succeed early in life and has been able to duplicate her accomplishments in various industries with impressive returns. It is only natural that she, as one who thrives on "likeability, trustability, and reliability," would detail her journey and formulas for achievement for others. Likewise, it is only natural that I, as one dedicated to motivating others to succeed, would endorse this book. Stacey and I, while operating in different arenas, share a common truth: help others achieve their dreams and you will achieve yours.

So the question now dear reader is this, do you want to succeed? Maybe you are one of those people who want to get ahead but don't know how to connect to those in a position to help. Perhaps you are on top of your field and are suddenly aware that your good fortune is beginning to wane. Rather still, are you someone just beginning in networking and looking for that special edge to start you on the right path? If any of these are true, you are in luck. If you can remain focused on your journey to greatness, then Stacey O'Byrne has provided a game plan, guide book, and testimonial to the path of overcoming setbacks and becoming a Master Networker.

Read on and aim high. - Les Brown

Preface

I have been in sales and marketing one way or another all my life. I have learned a lot of different styles and techniques; some great, some not so great. But one thing I have learned through my journey is that *people do business with people they like and trust*. That novel concept literally took only a second to learn, but an understanding that it is an ongoing journey to master. This concept is what I call the LTR Factor. The LTR Factor stands for Likeability + Trustabilty + Reliability = Referrability. Seems simple enough, right? However, this is a concept that few have mastered in order to most effectively leverage resources and convert their relationships to revenue.

Throughout my journey as a sales person, and as an entrepreneur, I learned very quickly how to leverage the LTR Factor. After honorably discharging from the military in my early 20's, I went on to do what I was "programmed" and expected to do by society. I went back to school, got a great education and pursued a career in corporate America. While climbing the ladder to success in sales, it quickly became apparent to me that buyers could and would buy from whoever they chose. A buyer's criteria was very simple; you had to have a competitive price, a quality product, be able to make their delivery date and, most importantly, they had to like and trust you. Simple, right? Wrong, so few sales people truly got this concept. Most sales people led with price, or fabricated the truth just a little to get that order. I stayed true to honoring the LTR Factor and by following this simple practice I quickly found myself making a very healthy six figure income in my early 20's. Suddenly, the industry I was in suffered extremely and deep cuts were made, including my job. I had become a casualty of 9/11. Unemployed and in shock, I had been totally blind sided and never saw it coming.

Preface

Unemployment turned out to be the biggest blessing for me. This was my pivotal moment and, although devastated at the time, I quickly embraced my situation and began my journey as an entrepreneur. A dear friend introduced me to business networking. Through the course of networking I was introduced to a business owner who was looking to shift his business and make some changes. Eventually we became business partners. Through strategic networking and building solid and mutually beneficial relationships, we took our business from $197,000 per year and $200,000 in debt to $1.2 million per year and lowered our debt to $187,000. This took 3½ years. Not bad, right? All of this was done by simply utilizing the principles of the LTR Factor.

Since being bitten by the entrepreneurial bug, I have utilized this concept to grow and develop two other businesses. Guess what? It worked again… and again! The second time I launched a business using the LTR Factor, and the "Secrets" that I am going to share with you, I started earning $20,000 to $30,000 per month within 3½ months. A few years ago was the launch of my sales and leadership training company, Pivot Point Advantage. First year sales, and in a down economy I might add, generated a nice six figure income; 100% from my networking efforts.

Dale Carnegie said it best, "*You can make more friends in two months by becoming interested in other people than you can in two years by trying to get other people interested in you.*" I love this quote. I believe that if you choose to live by these words and invest the time in developing and applying the right tools and planning, becoming a Master Networker will be inevitable.

Preface

As in anything, there are various levels to networking. Regardless if you are a beginner at networking, or if you have been networking for quite some time, you are just a few minor adjustments away from a path which leads you to success.

In this book I am going to share with you a fail-safe plan. No tricks, no gimmicks, just tried and true methods that work. Yes, that's right, actually WORK. You see, that is the second part of the word, netWORKING. It's not netSITTING, netCHATTING, netEATING, netGOSSIPING, netVISITING, netSOCIALIZING, netVOMMITING or netSELLING for that matter. It is **netWORKING**.

Networking is an art; a skill that gives you so much more leverage and advantage over your competition. If done properly, networking can set you apart from everyone else. The caveat being, **IF DONE PROPERLY**.

This is where so many fail. People do not understand that there is a right way and a wrong way to network.

*You can become
a Master Networker.*

1
How to Use This Book

I have written this book for you to use in developing your skills at networking so that you can become a Master Networker. Whether you are an entrepreneur, small business owner, executive or sales representative and whether you are new to networking or have been networking for years, I have included information and techniques to accommodate all skill levels and professions.

This book is your guide to developing a well-refined plan to establish and cultivate solid, successful, reciprocal relationships that you will reap benefits from for as long as you continue to do your due diligence. I have developed this to be an easy read, as well as for you to use as a workbook. This will help you develop a solid plan to guide you toward becoming a Master Networker and achieving success at this well-crafted art that we call networking. So whether you chose to write in this book, highlight it or you'd rather use a new notebook or journal, the important thing is to work the process.

I am not going to sugar coat this next statement because I believe in you that much. *Be true to yourself.* You bought this book for a reason; use it so you get the most out of your networking efforts. Don't be one of those people who has great intentions to improve something in their life that needs development, buys the tool that can help them, and then never utilizes it. Or worse yet, one who spends the time studying and reading something they have decided they wanted to improve or change in their life and then NEVER makes the necessary changes. Be true to the process and the process will be true to you! I have proven this method time and time again on my own businesses. Many small business owners, entrepreneurs and sales people have thoroughly worked this process with me and we are proof that this system works if you work the system. I look forward to you joining us through the journey of becoming a Master Networker and reaping the benefits of leveraging relationships and reciprocity to increase your revenue.

Just remember this, how you do the little things is how you do the big things, and how you do some things is how you do everything. I share this with you, because I have a belief that the effort we put forth in the littlest things in our lives is identical to the effort we will put forth towards the major things in our lives. It takes minimal effort to read this book; it takes more effort to do your due diligence in the exercises included in this book. If you poo-poo the process and effort here, that is the exact mirror image that you will put towards your effort in networking. So roll up your sleeves and dig in, you deserve the results, RIGHT?

Personally, I learn better by taking notes in a new notebook or journal and working from that. For me it is just easier. When I buy books to teach myself something, I have found that I like to read them over and over again. If I had written in the original book/workbook, it prevents me from learning something new or seeing something differently the next time I read it. This is just what I have found works best for me. Others learn best by writing and highlighting in their books. This is your book. This is your journey. Do what works best for you.

No Frills Delivery Approach

You will find that I am a very straightforward person and that is exactly how I am delivering this information to you. I am by no means the type of person to candy coat anything. People who know me know that just isn't my style. I mean what I say and I say what I mean. Some laugh and say I suffer from "NFS" (No Filter Syndrome).

You know, it is sad but true that no matter how badly we are failing our friends and families are always there to support us! They actually support us failing. I am not so sure that is a good thing. I am not saying failure is a bad thing. Honestly, I think failure provides us the feedback we need to make adjustments to create our successes. However, what I am saying is that our family and friends aren't always the most honest with us. They tell us how wonderful we are. They accept our excuses. They even help us create excuses as to why and what it is we are doing that is making things not work for us. Albert Einstein said it most eloquently, "The definition of insanity is doing the same thing over and over again and expecting different results." What I want to do is take you outside your realm of comfort because in doing so, you start to experience true personal growth and get different results.

The Program

This book is going to start by guiding you through building a solid foundation. Through this process you may ask yourself how this could possibly have anything to do with networking. You will later find that having a solid foundation and understanding has everything to do with the art of successful networking. Then, I will take you through identifying and cultivating the key relationships necessary to take you and your business to the next level. We will then address some fundamental necessities; some basic and some that aren't so basic. From there we move right into developing a steadfast networking plan for you to easily and successfully implement. All of these steps will take you on your journey to becoming a Master Networker.

This program was developed for all types of personalities. Regardless of whether you are a diehard introvert or a flamboyant extravert, this program is for you. This book doesn't have scripts in it to tell you what to say to who and when. Master Networkers live in the present and engage with each person authentically and congruently. Remember this important fact; *the key to successful relationships is authenticity* so the plan has to be 100% you and your own verbiage. Be true to yourself, and your plan will be true to you.

Networking is a skill; it is an art. I keep saying that because it is the truth. It is a skill because skills are developed and perfected with continual practice over time. It does not happen overnight. Networking is also an art because like all art of any modality, it involves finesse, authenticity and a high level of congruency. The only way to achieve congruency is through authenticity, and the only way to achieve authenticity is by being true to yourself. This may sound a little woo woo, but it's not meant to be. It is something I have found to be true to the art of successfully networking, building relationships and becoming a Master Networker.

Don't finish reading this book and expect to be able to give and receive a windfall of referrals. It doesn't work that way. A gold medalist will train for five to ten years every day of the week for just 60 seconds of perfection. Becoming a Master Networker is a journey, it is not a destination. The more you get yourself out there meeting new people, the more your database will grow. The more you work on understanding your database, the easier it will become to connect products, services and solutions with needs, wants and desires. Continue to do this with a plan and with laser focus and in no time you will find yourself being a Master Connector and quickly on your way to becoming a Master Networker.

Something important to keep in mind during your journey is there are three stages to learning:

1. Awkward
2. Mechanical
3. Natural

You will have to go through all three of these stages before you are comfortable. The more authentic you are to yourself, the more quickly you will reach a more natural stage.

I have been able to experience these stages of learning through the eyes of my daughter. She is in elementary school and I help her with her homework. A child in elementary school has to go through the awkward and mechanical processes of learning; how to read, write and do arithmetic, all of the basic knowledge that is so automatic for us that we take for granted today. It has given me the opportunity to truly understand and reflect back on the learning process. Do you remember when you learned how to read for the first time? It wasn't easy at all! How about basic algebra? That wasn't so basic in the beginning either.

Keep referring to this book as your guide to continually develop successful networking skills. As you and your business grow and develop, so will your plan. This plan should never be static; it should remain a living, breathing document that grows and develops along with you and your business.

Master Networker Tip #1
Be true to yourself and your plan will be true to you.

2

Terms of Endearment

With every new endeavor comes with it a set of new terminology. So, whether you are new to business networking, have dabbled in multiple networking environments, or even consider yourself a seasoned pro, there are several terms utilized that you may find it helpful to understand the meaning behind them. I have not only included words and their definitions that you will hear out there networking, but I am also going to include and define phraseology that is used in this book to better help you.

Let's start with defining the foundation of what it is we are doing and why.

Networking

Creating a group of acquaintances and associates and keeping it active through regular communication for mutual benefit. Networking is based on the question "How can I help?" and not with "What can I get?"

Word of Mouth Marketing (WOMM)

Oral or written recommendation by a satisfied customer to the prospective customers of a good or service. WOMM is considered to be the most effective form of promotion. It is also called word of mouth advertising which is incorrect because, by definition, advertising is a paid and non-personal communication.

Now that you have a better understanding what it is you are doing out there, let's focus on the definitions of what it is you are out there seeking.

CART

A Law that all Master Networkers live by. Congruency, Authenticity, Reciprocity and Transparency.

Centers of Influence

Influential people within a community. These are people who have significant databases and know others that would be good prospects and/or connections for you. Typically this is another business professional.

Commercial (a.k.a. Elevator Ptich)

A short summary used to quickly and simply define a product, service, or organization and its value proposition. The name "elevator pitch" reflects the idea that it should be possible to deliver the summary in the time span of an elevator ride, or approximately thirty seconds to two minutes. A well designed commercial should sum up unique aspects of your product or service in a way that excites others.

Congruent

The state achieved by coming together, the state of agreement, harmony, conformity, and alignment.

Customer Relationship Manager (CRM)

Processes implemented by a company to handle its database management and contact with its customers.

Leverage

Ability to influence a system, or an environment, in a way that multiplies the outcome of one's efforts without a corresponding increase in the consumption of resources. In other words, leverage is an advantageous condition of having a relatively small amount of cost which yields a relatively high level of returns. Thus, "doing a lot with a little."

LTR Factor

The recipe for success as it applies to referability. LTR stands for Likeability, Trustability and Reliability. By mastering the LTR Factor it streams lines the referral and relationship processes.

Master

Maestro: an artist of consummate skill. One whose teachings or doctrines are accepted by followers. An artist or performer of great and exemplary skill. An expert.

Reciprocal

Relationship in which an act or movement of one party is met (or countered) with a corresponding act or movement of the other.

Referral

The act of telling someone about the positive features of a person or a business. Connecting a need, want or desire with a product, service or solution.

Referral Partner Meetings (RPMs)

Productive face-to-face meetings or tele-meetings designed to help Referral Partners and Strategic Referral Partners better get to know each other and to educate each other on how and who to refer.

Relationship Marketing

Promotional and selling activities aimed at developing and managing trusting and long-term relationships with larger customers. Customer profile, buying patterns, and history of contacts is maintained in a sales database, and a service representative (also called account executive) is assigned to one or more major customers to fulfill their needs and maintain the relationship.

Referral Worksheet

A tool used to organize and communicate necessary information to a Referral Partner / Strategic Power Partner that will best help them help you. This tool at a minimum should communicate what an ideal prospect/referral/client is for you, what a good Strategic Power Partner is for you, what it is they should look for, and what is it they should listen for.

Return on Investment (ROI)

A metric used to measure rates of return on dollars invested in an economic entity. ROI provides a snapshot of profitability adjusted for the size of the investment assets tied up in the enterprise. Marketing decisions have obvious potential connection to the numerator of ROI (profits). Marketers should understand the position of their company and the returns expected. ROI is often compared to expected (or required) rates of return on dollars invested.

Strategic Power Partner

The most strategic of Referral Partners. This Referral Partner is the epitome of Pareto Principle, the 80/20 rule. A Strategic Power Partner has the same target market as you; which makes their ability to refer to you, effortless.

Strategic PowerPartner Management (SPPM)

A process put into place to best manage your most coveted Referral Partner.

Target Market

A group of customers that a business has decided to aim its marketing efforts towards. A well-defined target market is the first element to a marketing strategy. Target markets are groups of individuals separated by distinguishable and noticeable aspects. Target markets can be separated into:

- Geographic segmentations, addresses
  (their location climate region)

- Demographic/socioeconomic segmentation (gender, age, income, occupation, education, household size, and stage in the family life cycle)
- Psychographic segmentation (similar attitudes, values, and lifestyles)
- Behavioral segmentation (occasions, degree of loyalty)
- Product-related segmentation (relationship to a product)

These words and their meanings will serve you well through your journey of becoming a Master Networker. The more to heart you take their definitions, the more engrained becoming a Master Networker becomes in your DNA. Being a Master Networker is truly a shift in mindset.

Your Center of Influence

This is your ever increasing database which you have varying degrees of impact in your ability to refer products, services and solutions to needs, wants and desires. This is your ever increasing social currency.

There are a few other words and their meanings that I find important for you to become familiar with, not only through reading this book but also while you are out there growing your referral empire.

Master Networker Tip #2
Have a complete understanding of
what it is you are seeking,
what it is you want, and
what it is you have to offer.

3

How the Process
Came to Fruition

As I had shared earlier, shortly after September 11, 2001, I was laid off from a very comfortable corporate job which I had held for 15 years. I found myself lost and unsure as to what I was going to do with my life. The industry I was in was downsizing every other month after that historic tragedy. The skill sets I had developed were primarily focused in sales and leadership. I held a management position in a niche industry. The relationships I had established were only professionally valuable for me if I had remained in that industry.

So, I found myself doing what a significant percentage of America, at that time was doing; putting together my resume and searching for a "job." I did everything I was supposed to do. I contacted key people in the industry, submitted my resume to multiple different online websites, checked the newspaper daily, called competitors and reached out to a lot of customers I had established relationships with over the past 15 years. I went from being a successful, strong six figure income earner, to unemployed and over-qualified in a market that was pivotal for many businesses and industries.

Months went by and it was definitely taking its toll on my confidence. I guess you could say I was allowing my net worth define my self worth. My dear friend Althea was an entrepreneur, coming from "the corporate world" that was very intriguing and impressive to me. One of the businesses she was starting was a networking group. She had been trying to get me out of the house for weeks to go to one of these networking meetings with her. If only you could have been in my mind at the time. Not knowing and understanding what business networking was, I had one of two scenarios going through my mind every time she called me to go with her.

Scenario #1

Scenario #1 was a room full of IT people talking about computers, software and servers. This definitely was not my type of environment or conversation. In the type of career I came from, Networking / IT was a department all of its own. I knew my computer had a button, and if something was wrong, I picked up the phone, called the guys in IT, and they networked into my computer and fixed it. Problem solved. I just had no desire to insert myself into a room full of computer people and talk about computer networking. It was a topic and a language I knew nothing about. Since Althea was a computer software trainer she would have a lot in common with them and I would be left alone.

Scenario #2

Scenario #2 is where my mind continued to drift because it was more of what I understood and had personally experienced in my corporate career. Networking in the industry I had come from, as well as had gained all of my professional experience from, was fun, and it was easy. We went to expos, trade shows or customer parties. We would buy as many cocktails as necessary for our customers and manufacture reps to find out who the top sales people were at our competitors, then proceed to buy those top sales people as many cocktails as necessary for them to say yes to our job offer. Business done, sales would increase and relationships were mastered! I was so down and frustrated from job hunting, I just wasn't in the mood to "party" or drink.

One morning, Althea, persistent as she was, called me and gave me no choice. She was coming to pick me up at 11 a.m., ready or not, and it would behoove me to be professionally dressed because she was dragging me with her no matter what I was wearing. I knew her all too well. If I was still in my PJ's she would drag me all the way there kicking and screaming.

This was the day that would forever change my life. Fearfully I did as I was told. I donned my best professional attire and reluctantly awaited her car to pull up in my driveway. Sure enough, you can set your watch by her, and at 11 a.m. there she was, honking her horn in my driveway.

I got in her car and she started to talk to me. She was telling me:

- Where we were going
- What I should expect
- Who would be there
- Who I would probably want to connect with and why
- What I will need to do after I leave

I have to be honest, all I heard was blah, blah, blah, blah and was so lost. Remember Scenerios #1 and #2? I had no clue what I was in for, nor any idea what to expect. All I knew was how persistent Althea was and would continue to be if I didn't get out of the house. Her heart was in the right place, she meant well and just wanted to help me, but honestly, I was just going so she would get off my back because I FINALLY got out of the house!

We walked into a restaurant; to a separate private room in the back. To my surprise there was no bar and no alcohol. Instead there were 75 people mingling and talking with each other. I turned around and "poof" the friend that brought me there was gone. So I went and found a wall to hold up and stood there in amazement, watching all these people talk with each other. The buzz in the room was electrifying, almost magnetic. It was very entertaining to watch, yet extremely intimidating. To see it from the eyes of a spectator was truly amazing. Knowing what I know now and having the opportunity to reflect back is a gift. All the different dynamics involved. All the different personalities involved. I can't forget to mention all the people trying to out-sell each other and make sure that any money in the room ended up in their own pocket.

Several minutes into holding up the wall, I was approached by a very nice older woman. All I remember was that she was trying to sell me something. She shoved her business card into my hand and wanted a business card from me. I explained to her I didn't have a business card because I didn't have a "job" and as for buying something from her, well I didn't have a "job." Seconds later she left me to myself holding up the wall again. I found myself thinking how odd her approach was because if she had just spent a few more minutes with me, she would have given me the opportunity to tell her I knew somebody that needed, wanted and would buy what it was that she was selling. But she didn't stick around long enough for me to tell her and I certainly wasn't leaving that wall. It might fall down!

A few minutes later Althea found me, grabbed my hand and dragged me into the middle of this cattle call environment. In case you haven't noticed by now, I am an introvert through and through. I have always been very good at sales but through my own techniques, building solid relationships and trust. The next thing I knew I was surrounded by all of these business professionals and she was introducing me. They were all handing me their business cards, shaking my hand, telling me what they did and asking me what I did; which I have to admit I thought was pretty rude and bold to be asking a perfect stranger what it is they did to earn money. Even more so since it was extremely embarrassing to admit that I was unemployed while being surrounded by all these sales people, business owners and entrepreneurs. Looking back on it now I realize how completely clueless I was, but I am grateful for that experience because it truly opened my eyes to several things; how valuable networking could be, how not to network and how important it is to show up in service by tuning into WIIFT (what's in it for them) and not WIIFM (what's in it for me).

I must have left there with over 50 business cards in my hand, not really knowing what to do with them. The days to follow I received many soliciting phone calls and emails from people who had given me their business cards and in return had asked me for my contact info, which Althea had so generously written on the back of her business cards and given them out on my behalf. It was pretty frustrating. I didn't have a JOB, why didn't they get that? The last thing I needed was for people I didn't know trying to sell me something I didn't think I needed. If I had a JOB I could afford what they were selling, but then again if I had a JOB I probably would have never been there, in that environment, getting bit by the *networking bug*.

Despite the fact that my experience was somewhat negative and a little violating, there was something about it, something about the electricity and magnetism that intrigued me. There was something about this networking thing that was very fascinating to me. I loved the energy in the room; the people that went to these meetings were so nice. I had to go back; I had to get my friend to take me again. So I did, again and again, and my life as an entrepreneur and business owner was born. I had been bitten by the entrepreneurial bug! I had learned very valuable lessons that day. I learned that networking does not entail just showing up at an event and collecting as many business cards as possible. And believe it or not, networking is not joining a group or groups and never showing up either. There is so much more to networking. It's kind of like having a gym membership and never going to the gym, or even utilizing your membership and going to the gym but just sitting there and never using any of the equipment or weights. Will you get good results, let alone any? This is why networking is an art. Networking is a skill that, if practiced and taken seriously, will allow you to reap the rewards for years to come.

I believe that in order to understand how something best works, it helps to understand how something doesn't work. So, how does somebody network wrong? I often refer to these examples as "The Networking Disconnect." Here are a few examples of how **NOT** to network:

1. Have you ever been at a networking event, mixer, expo or convention and had someone shove their product, service, or idea in your face? After they shove their business card or brochure in your face, they start **netVOMMITTING** their sales

pitch on you as if you showed interest in buying what it is they are selling. This is not **netWORKING** this is netVOMMITTING and netSELLING!

2. How about the person that pays their entry fee into a meeting or event, walks in and grabs a plate of food then sits down and starts eating? This isn't networking either. This is **netEATING**. Or the person that goes straight to the bar and starts drinking, this is **netDRINKING**.

3. What about the person, who walks in, sees their friends, walks over and they all start talking about their family, kids and weekend? Then when it is time to sit down for the meeting, they all go over and sit together. Guess what, this isn't networking either, this would be considered **netSITTING, netCHATTING** or **netVISITING**.

We have all seen these behaviors in action, at meetings and events. If we are completely honest with ourselves, we have all done one or all of these blunders at some point or another during our networking efforts.

Networking is an art that requires a particular skill set. Developing and practicing these skills to become a Master Networker will assist you in growing your credibility, reputation, database and business in a multitude of ways. Networking can and will open doors for you; which in some cases may never have been opened, or in other cases, taken a very long time just to get through the gatekeeper. Networking can prevent your competition from taking key customers away from you because you have become such a valued asset and connection resource, that you have ultimately become an extended partner of their business. Proper networking also gives you the opportunity to grow your business at a faster rate because you have more "feet on the street" representing you and your business. All this and much more are the benefits of skillful networking.

I refer to these advantages as leverage. The dictionary defines **leverage** as:

1. Positional advantage; power to act effectively.
2. To improve or enhance.
3. Strategic advantage; power to act effectively; "relatively small groups can sometimes exert immense leverage."

I define **leverage as NETWORKING**. Networking is the ability to authentically build and cultivate strong and mutually beneficial relationships.

Think about it. We have been building relationships of some kind all of our lives. Ask yourself, which relationships were the most successful? Which relationships lasted the longest? If you really look back on them, the answers are usually pretty much the same. The relationships that tend to last the longest and are the most successful are the relationships which allowed you to be your most authentic self, they were mutually beneficial, and they were continually cultivated.

Have you ever been to a meeting or an event and watched somebody walk into the room and they "owned it"? I don't mean they carried a high level of arrogance. I mean that you could just feel their presence, their energy? People "noticed" them, flocked to them, wanted to connect with them? Everything about them was electric, magnetic. They oozed servitude not attitude. That is a Master Networker. A Master Networker means what they say and says what they mean. A Master Networker is a person of value. A Master Networker is a person who "gets it" as very few do. A Master Networker is a person who offers value to other people's businesses and shows up at a level of service without the intent to sell.

To help make this even clearer, let's take a look at some alternative networking styles. How about the person who walks into the room and few people really notice them? They kind of blend in with the masses; they become part of the crowd. What about the netSELLER? These people are loud and obnoxious. They scan the group looking for their next victim with a smoking checkbook or credit card? Or, how about the networker who shows up to be everyone's friend as if it was social hour or happy hour? Now is the time to ask yourself, which type of networker do I want to be?

Networking is the pivotal foundation of success in growing your business; that is when the art of networking is mastered. In this book we will focus on developing all skills that will allow you to become that Master Networker. This book will help you to create the ability necessary for successfully planning, practicing, implementing and cultivating your way to networking success. If you stay true to yourself and this process, you will experience levels of success you had only ever hoped and dreamed of.

Through my journey as a business owner/entrepreneur, I have learned that networking is not only an art and a skill, but a very important part of a small business's sales, marketing and advertising plan. With today's small business owner being stretched so thin, frequently referred to as CEO (Chief Everything Officer), and cash reserves potentially strapped or non-existent, they need to ensure that they get the biggest bang for their buck, both in time and money. We need to market, but how do we differentiate ourselves from our competition? We need to advertise, but how and where, not to mention where are the financial resources going to come from? In case you didn't notice, I used that "plan" word again, when I mentioned advertising plan. The sooner a small business owner and an entrepreneur realizes growing business doesn't happen by accident, nor by throwing everything out there to see what sticks, the sooner they will save time and money and enjoy the success of their efforts because of their solid, effective networking plan.

I have been told over the years that I am an amazing connector and have helped people secure business that they might not have ever had. That's right, I help people secure business. That is one of the most important steps in your journey to becoming a Master Networker, to help others make the necessary connections that will assist them in securing new business. I believe that your relationships, or as I like to refer to them as your "social currency", directly impacts your net worth. I am not saying that the more affluent the people are that you interface with will directly impact your bank account, although that does help. What I am saying is that you need to understand that your relationships, both personal and professional, create your database or your Center of Influence. Your understanding of the needs, wants and desires of your Center of Influence as well as their products, services and solutions; can very easily help you become a Master Connector. By adding that much value to a relationship you become a significant Center of Influence. When you authentically show up in a space of service and truly care about making an impact in someone's life or business, then they will ultimately want to do the same for you. This is the beginning of your journey to becoming a Master Networker.

Seems simple enough, networking that is. Find a meeting or a mixer, show up, pay admission, meet people, talk, eat and leave. That's easy? Right? If it is that easy, why do so many people complain about not getting anything out of their networking group, or out of a meeting or out of networking itself for that matter?

Defined, business networking is the process of establishing a mutually beneficial relationship with other business people, potential clients and/or customers. Notice that I don't say anything about meeting people in this definition, which seems to be the ever-increasing slew of business networking meet-and-greet events that has given business networking a bad name. The key to true business networking is the establishment of a mutually beneficial relationship. And that's an incredibly rare event considering the standard shake-hands-and-exchange-your-business-card events that are touted as business networking "opportunities".

You will find that the best business Networking Groups operate as exchanges of business information, ideas, and support. The opportunity to "connect" is provided. It is what you do before you get there, while you are there, and after you leave that truly define successful networking.

Master Networker Tip #3

Listening – Focusing on how you can help the person you are listening to rather than on how he or she can help you is the first step to establishing a mutually beneficial relationship.

4

Who Are You
When Nobody is Watching?
Is Who You Need to Be
When Everybody is Watching?

Who you are when nobody is watching is exactly who you should be when everybody is watching. Knowing and understanding yourself is an important key to successful networking. No, I'm not going to get all therapeutic on you. You don't need to call your therapist for analysis. You just need to be true to yourself. Knowing and understanding yourself gives you the opportunity to put yourself in environments that are congruent to who you are and allow you to stay within a zone that lets you be authentic and not fake. As one of my mentors, Andi Burgis, constantly tells me, "1% incongruent is incongruent." This phrase is very powerful when it comes to doing business, any kind of business, especially business that relies on relationships. It's kind of like pregnancy. You aren't kind of pregnant or a little pregnant. You either are or you are not. Same applies to congruency, you either are or you are not. *No matter what you do, be true to yourself and by all means make sure you love what you do.*

The C.A.R.T. System

There is a law out there that Master Networkers embrace and honor. It is called the C.A.R.T. System. Like any other law, it can be broken, but if a law is broken there are always consequences. This is a key ingredient to the becoming a Master Networker and mastering the LTR Factor; likeability, trustability, reliability equates to referability. In order to incorporate the C.A.R.T. System into your business and your life you have to have an understanding of the principles and the laws.

C = The Law of Congruency

The definition of congruency is *agreement, harmony, conformity, alignment.*

This is your why. Why are you doing what it is you are doing? It will not serve you to be surface level here. You want to get real and you need to get deep. You have to be in complete alignment with what you are doing. If not, you won't be able to communicate the emotion attached to your product, service or solution. Emotion is a very important factor in relationships. (In fact, I would go so far as to say this is THE MOST important factor in relationships.) A key factor to be aware of is that the word 'motion' is a key part of the word 'emotion'. Emotion creates motion, motion creates action and action creates results. I believe that our gut is the smartest brain in our body. When someone is lacking their why, lacking their congruency in what it is they do and who it is they are, they send off energy, or a vibration, that lands in a very negative manner in our gut. This is when that red light start flashing and all the signals go off to be aware of danger. Have you ever gone against your gut? Need I say more?

A = The Law of Authenticity

The definition of authenticity is *conforming to fact and therefore worthy of trust, reliance, or belief.*

Business people today "show up" how they think people expect them to be as opposed to showing up as themselves. People will show up wearing a proverbial mask, so to speak. The problem with this concept is simple. People do business with people they like and trust. If you are networking with someone and you are "wearing this mask" so that you are who you think they want you to be, it is only a matter of when, not if, that the real you will show up. This usually happens about the time you start getting comfortable and you let your guard down. Then out of the blue the person you have been building a business relationship with suddenly finds themselves interfacing with a stranger. This creates an environment of doubt and mistrust. It is important to be you and to be comfortable being you. Remember… people do business with people they like and trust. People will like you and trust you quicker if you allow them to get to know the real you.

R = The Law of Reciprocity

The definition of reciprocity is *the exchange, recognition, privileges or obligations between two or more people, mutual respect and mutual benefit.*

This is another important piece of the pie. You know the old adage, "What goes around comes around. " That applies to good or bad. Some key factors to be aware of in the definition are: it is a privilege to have the opportunity to learn about someone and their business; it is an obligation to add value to that relationship; and essential to ensure that it is understood that it must be mutually beneficial.

T = The Law of Transparency

The definition of transparency is *free from pretense or deceit, easily detected or seen through, sheer enough to be seen through.*

Have you ever been in a conversation with someone during a networking meeting or event and they seem to be asking you questions that have an ulterior motive attached to them? I will share with you an example. You are having a pleasant conversation, during the meet and greet portion of a networking meeting, with someone who sells a product that reduces/relieves pain, we will call him Joe. As you are having casual conversation, Joe starts asking questions that may seem innocent but really have a motif attach to them. He could possibly ask you if you have any kids, seems pretty innocent doesn't it. Through the course of answering that innocent question, he may throw out another one, are they in soccer. You braggingly answer, "Yes, we just had practice last night. I'll tell you what though; I am not as young as I used to be. I played around with the team yesterday during practice and could barely get out of bed this morning. Guess what just happened. Bam, you have been steered into the perpetual corner of netSELLING and netVOMMITTING purgatory and it all started out so innocent. Joe has you now, he has been trained to hear certain buzz words. He really wasn't sharing in pleasantries with you to get to know you and become a potential Referral Partner, he was steering you with questions, to see if you fell into his potential target market. This scenario can happen with any product or service and frankly, we have all been Joe once or twice in our life. If you have found yourself in this scenario, which based on my experience I am certain that you have, there is a high probability that the person you are talking with has an ulterior motive. Their industry has taught them that there are certain buzz words and catch phrases that they should listen for and as soon as they hear them, BAM! they got you. You just admitted that you had a need, want or desire for their product and now they can netSELL and netVOMIT all over you! The Law of Transparency allows you to establish a sacred space of possibility. This establishes an environment of, "what you see is what you get." It allows for you to engage in a conversation with no hidden agenda.

The CART System is extremely powerful. Each element/law within itself is a very powerful resource/tool that when tapped into allows the possibility to achieve high levels of success. However, when all the laws are combined and enacted together the CART System is the true recipe for success. If any one of these elements is compromised at any time, it is impossible to establish the type of professional relationships necessary to leverage the true power networking has to offer.

Knowing and understanding yourself as it applies to networking is important because if you stick yourself in an environment that you aren't comfortable in, that you have nothing in common with, or have no relation to who and what you are, then you are doing yourself, your wallet and your time a huge injustice. If you are uncomfortable, then you are sending out an uncomfortable vibe and will not be as approachable, trustable or likeable. You will be awkward, and it will be that awkwardness that will prevent people from being drawn to you. Let's just say for example, that you are not comfortable dressing in professional suits. You find this meeting that everyone has told you is totally amazing. You have been advised to dress for success because the attendees are extremely successful and dress in very expensive suits. You show up exactly how you were told, in your best professional attire, and sure enough you find yourself very uncomfortable. This just isn't you. Unfortunately, because of your discomfort, you are vibrating an energy that is showing up as incongruent or unauthentic. So the people you are meeting aren't really sure why they don't want to get to know you. Something just doesn't feel right for them. This is definitely the type of situation you need and want to avoid, especially when you are walking into a meeting for the first time. It's unfortunate but true, first impressions are lasting. Make sure that you understand yourself well enough to know what environments you are comfortable inserting yourself into and which might not be a great idea, especially until you become a seasoned networker.

If you find that you are not comfortable walking into a networking meeting or event alone, then go with people you know. There is nothing wrong with attending networking meetings with a few people. It is actually a strategy that we will get into later, but most importantly there are strengths in numbers and going with a friend, co-worker, professional acquaintance or group of people is comforting. You then know you are not alone and if for whatever reason you get uncomfortable then you can fall back to someone you know and regroup. But do not, and I repeat, do not stay with them the whole meeting. You are there to work.

It is very important to know and understand your personality. There are many different personality and behavioral style assessments out there. I highly recommend taking an assessment, or at least educating yourself about the four major styles, so you understand exactly what type of personality you are, what type of personality you attract and what type of personality you repel. You can also identify what sales personality type you are. This will help you understand how you will best thrive in a networking environment. Are you outgoing? Can you walk up to anybody and just start talking no matter what? Are you shy, introverted, the one that helps hold up the wall? Are you the techy type who wants to talk about the intricate workings of things? Do you just love to make friends with everybody you meet? Are you a front-of-the-room kind of person, or a behind-the-scenes kind of person, or a team player? Knowing this is important to the role you will play in networking. Knowing and understanding your personality type will help you choose Networking Groups and environments that fit your comfort level. It will help you understand how you naturally approach and communicate with other people and most importantly how you show up in other people's eyes.

Through this process of understanding yourself, it is also important to identify what your strengths and weaknesses are as a person. As I keep saying, people do business with people they like and trust. This being said, you will want to identify what personality traits you have that will attract people to you, as well as what is important for you to focus on improving and developing. For some people, identifying strengths is pretty easy; it's our weaknesses, or our "opportunities for improvement", that we have a harder time seeing. For others it is the direct opposite. They can rattle off a hundred weaknesses but can't mention any strengths.

Exercise I

Spend some serious quiet time with yourself and make a list of your top five strengths and your top five weaknesses or as I like to refer to them as "opportunities for improvement".

Individual Perception of Strengths

1. _____

2. _____

3. _____

4. _____

5. _____

Individual Perception of Weaknesses/Opportunities

1. _____

2. _____

3. _____

4. _____

5. _____

Now that you have taken a self-inventory and identified your strengths and opportunities for improvement, I suggest sitting down with a few people you truly trust and ask them to be brutally honest with you. Ask them to share with you what they perceive to be your personal strengths and personal weaknesses/opportunities.

Outside Perception of Strengths

1. _____

2. _____

3. _____

4. _____

5. _____

Outside Perception of Weaknesses/Opportunities

1. _____

2. _____

3. _____

4. _____

5. _____

After you have this list, come up with different ways to improve these weaknesses. You see, our weaknesses are one of our strongest assets. When you see what it is you can develop and improve about yourself and take *action* upon, it just makes you that much more valuable. Continually developing yourself is one of the stepping stones to success.

Opportunities for Improvement

1. _____

   a. How to improve _____

2. _____

   a. How to improve _____

3. _____

   a. How to improve _____

4. _____

   a. How to improve _____

5. _____

   a. How to improve _____

Master Networker Tip #4
Be Yourself, Be Authentic. People do business with people they like and trust. If you aren't being yourself, how will they ever get to know you enough to trust and like you?

5

Know and Understand Your Business

So at this point you are probably thinking to yourself, I am my business. I just did a personal discovery exercise in Chapter 4, I now know and understand myself. Why do I have to do this again? You see, no matter what role you play in your business, your business is not just an extension of you. It is a separate entity, which means the business takes on its own personality. It is capable of attracting and repelling its own type of clientele and frankly, it has its own needs. Don't get me wrong, your business is an extension of you, and it always will be a reflection of who you are. It's just that it also has its own separate identity that can and will appeal and repel different people.

So let's start dissecting your business. Now is the time you want to pull out your business plan and marketing plan and dust them off. This is the true beginning of networking. Yes, that is right, before you ever walk out that door and into a networking meeting, it is very important you have an understanding of your business and your industry. It is important to know the direction you want to take your business, the reputation of your industry and how other industries and businesses might perceive it. It is important to know the capabilities of your business and its strengths and growth opportunities. What are good clients? What are bad clients? What are great referrals? What are great referral sources?

The first thing you want to look at is your target market? *What type of industry/prospect most needs, wants or desires your product/service/*

idea? The Target Market for your business is where you focus your energy, it's your sweet spot.

Your target market is those most likely to buy from you. Do yourself a favor and don't be too general with the hopes of getting a larger slice of the pie. That's like standing in front of a target and going READY-SHOOT-AIM. It doesn't work and if anything, it's expensive and jeopardizes the vitality of your business. To be a Master Networker, you must know and understand yourself, your business and your prospective Target Market. Preparation is key! The dollars are in the details!

Try to describe your target market with as much detail as you can, based on your knowledge of your product or service. Rope your family and friends into visualization exercises. Ask them questions like "Describe the typical person who'll hire me to paint their kitchen to make it look like marble". In order to get different perspectives, the more people you ask the better.

Here are some questions to get you started:

If Your Focus is Business to Consumer
- Are your target customers male or female?
- How old are they?

- Where do they live? Is geography a limiting factor for any reason?
- What do they do for a living?
- How much money do they make?
- What other aspects of their lives matter?

If Your Focus is Business to Business
- Are your target customers large corporations or small businesses?
- How long have they been in existence?
- Where are they located in relation to your business? Is geography a limiting factor for any reason?
- What is their annual revenue?
- How many employees do they have?
- What else is relevant about their business?

Target Market

1. _____

2. _____

3. _____

4. _____

5. _____

So now that you have your target market clear, let's take a look at your ideal clients. Who are they? What do they do? What about them is so appealing and ideal to you and your business? Get very clear on these specifics. Whether you have a list of company names, or a list of personality types / characteristics, this is information you are going to need in the near future. So the more specific you are now, the easier it is going to be for you later. Whether you have a product, service or idea, and regardless of whether your focus is business to consumer or business to business, you have an ideal client. The more specific you get, the better it will be for moving forward in your networking ventures.

List Your Ideal Client

1. _____

2. _____

3. _____

4. _____

5. _____

Is your list as ideal as it can be? Did you use the words: anybody, somebody or everybody? Were you loose or broad in defining? How specific were you? Were you specific enough that if you handed your list to someone who didn't know you they could walk away and bring you a few of your ideal clients immediately? Let's use one of my favorite examples as to what your list should not look like. Let's say you were a chiropractor. You shared with me your ideal client was "anybody with a spine." I can tell you immediately that no one came to mind. However, I did visualize several spineless people I have met in the past. If you view it from this perspective, not everyone with a spine needs a chiropractor. I live in Southern California, when it rains people seem to forget how to drive. You would think it was snowing out with the amount of accidents that happen on our freeways during the rainy season. So with that in mind, let's take a look at how the chiropractor can better describe to us their ideal client. "A great referral for me would be a person who has been in a car accident within the past couple months and they are experiencing lower back pain, stiffness or neck pain." When we are that specific in what we are looking for, it is that much easier for people to connect us to who we want to meet. Consider this, if you can't specifically describe who you want then how can someone go out and find them for you?

You have now specifically identified your target market as well as your ideal client. Now we get to identify what the strengths and weaknesses are of your business. It is very important to understand your capabilities. Despite what we think or choose to believe, we cannot be everything to everybody. So by understanding our strengths and weaknesses, we will be able to best describe what a great referral is for our business and what a bad referral is for our business.

As you did when you identified strengths and weaknesses for yourself, you now need to identify them for your business. This is going to be a little more difficult. We are so passionate about what we do, that we have the hardest time identifying the areas we are weakest in.

The whole point of this exercise is so when you go out there, you can speak very confidently and specifically about what you offer. So you don't just hit somebody with a list of offerings so long and so in depth that they are left feeling confused because all they heard was blah blah blah. We have all been on both ends of the conversation. You want to be concise; there truly is merit in those 60 second elevator speeches and yes, we will work on 60 second commercials in detail in another chapter.

When you identify your weaknesses, you have the opportunity to put together a plan for improvement because you honestly took the time and evaluated your business needs. Remember, if you were true to this process, they are not weaknesses, they are opportunities.

As for the strengths of your business, if you are in manufacturing, this could be a product you do best, most frequently, and at the highest level of quality, efficiency and price. If you have a business where you offer somebody else's product, well then identify their most popular product offering such as the hottest sellers. If you offer a service, then what is your most popular service? And last but not least, if you are completely new and don't have a history to fall back on, then this is going to be the product, service or idea which you have invested the most time, energy and effort into developing, offering and supporting. This gives you the ability to offer the highest levels of quality and service at the most competitive price to your market. Take some time to be true to this process and identify both the strengths and opportunities of your business.

Business Strengths

1. _____

2. _____

3. _____

4. _____

5. _____

Business Weaknesses/Opportunities

1. _____

2. _____

3. _____

4. _____

5. _____

Now that you have identified the weaknesses of your business, you have an opportunity to improve your business by focusing in on and developing these areas. This really has nothing to do with networking and everything to do with good sound business practices; which ultimately has everything to do with networking. Always refining and improving yourself and your business is of extreme importance. This is what differentiates the successful from the struggling. Remember, our weaknesses are our strongest asset. It's when you see what it is you can develop and improve about your business, and then take action upon, that makes you that much more valuable.

Never stop developing and improving on both yourself and your business. An important philosophy to remember is; what you feed will grow and what you starve will die. I guarantee that if you aren't developing and improving, your competitor is and it is just a matter of time before they flourish in your market and you shrivel up and die.

Opportunities for Improvement

1. _____

   a. How to improve _____

2. _____

   a. How to improve _____

3. _____

   a. How to improve _____

4. _____

   a. How to improve _____

5. _____

   a. How to improve _____

You have now identified some very important factors which will make moving forward a lot easier.

You better understand what you and your business can and can't do. This clarity should assist you in better communicating who you are and what you do.

Master Networker Tip #5

Know and understand yourself, your business and your prospective target market. Do the work now before you ever walk out the door. It will save you both time and money.

6

Understanding the Different Referral Sources

Referral sources come in all different types, but they all have one common denominator and that is a strong foundation of trust based on a well established relationship.

Now that you have done your due diligence in identifying your target market, you want to look at who your potential referral sources are.

A referral source is exactly what it sounds like. This is a person or business that will play a powerful role in your future success by opening doors, making connections and introductions. We can even go as far to say that a few of these referral sources are going to become such strong allies that they will become your referral partners. No, they aren't going to own part of your business. However, if you have the right referral partners, they will act as if they are part of your business by the vested interest they take in helping you grow.

The Strategic Alliance

The first type of business you should consider taking a look at is your competitor. You know the old adage, "Keep your friends close and your enemies closer." Not all of your competitors are going to be your enemies. In this particular case, they would have the potential of becoming a strategic alliance.

Make a list of competitors that are within a reasonable circumference of your general area. After you are finished with the list, sort it by those that are larger than you and those that are smaller than you.

List 5 Competitors Who Are Too Small to Compete with Your Target Market

1. _____

2. _____

3. _____

4. _____

5. _____

List 5 Competitors Who Are Too Large to Compete with Your Target Market

1. _____

2. _____

3. _____

4. _____

5. _____

I am a firm believer that we need to completely understand our competition in order to differentiate ourselves from them. Your knowledge of your competition will determine how hard or easy this next exercise will be for you. After separating them by size, cross off the ones that don't have the same business beliefs as you. Whether it is quality, service, ethics, reputation or whatever else it is that defines and identifies your business, your brand. Whoever is left, is the beginning of your potential strategic alliance list.

Potential Strategic Alliance List

1. _____

2. _____

3. _____

4. _____

5. _____

You will have a different type of referral relationship with Strategic Alliance Partners than you will with other referral sources and Strategic Referral Partners, however, this relationship will still be based on similar concepts.

With these potential strategic alliance partners, you want to identify if they are interested in pursuing a mutually beneficial, strategic relationship with you. You may or may not know them, but now is as good a time as any to make the connection. You know what is too small and too large for you. You know what makes sense for you to pursue and what doesn't. For me, having a strategic relationship with a friendly competitor is a win - win for all involved; you, your competition, as well as existing and future clients.

For the competitors who are smaller than you, building a strategic alliance with them will allow you to offer a qualified competent source for business that you would otherwise turn down for being too small. Trust me when I tell you that nobody likes to be told their business is too small for you. However, if you explain to them that you are unable to properly service their specific need, but that you have a relationship with an industry partner that can and will be able to help them out, this person will forever remember you as a valuable source regardless of whether they are a current client or future one.

In return, when the smaller competitor gets something that is too big for them, they will refer the business to you. This works the same way but in reverse with the larger competitor.

This concept and philosophy doesn't work for every industry and it doesn't work for every business. It is a concept that if it can be worked out and managed, will open up a whole new realm of opportunities. So, consider whether or not it can work for you and your business. It is definitely an outside the box approach, and it requires a lot of trust between both parties to ensure that businesses don't attempt to steal each other's clients.

The Believer Referral Source

Just by putting yourself out there doing business daily and building credibility, you are developing a network of referral sources for yourself. There is a key word there and that is CREDIBILITY. Remember a very important rule from earlier, people do business with people they like and trust. This applies to referring to people as well, and possibly more so. People have to know you, believe in you, and trust you in order for them to introduce you to their loved ones, as well as their hard-earned clientele and center of influence.

You may not realize it, but you have referral sources within your existing clientele. Think about it, who better to wave your banner than an existing client who is continually happy with you, with what you do for them, and the level of service you provide for them! Some professionals have a difficult time asking their clients to refer them. They feel as if they are infringing on their clients or, if the client really wanted to refer them, that they would have already done so. That isn't always true. In most cases, it doesn't even dawn on them that something as simple as a referral or an introduction could be that powerful for you. They are distracted by their own business activities and concerns and aren't thinking about what you might need. Sometimes it just takes a simple request, which you will find in most cases they are happy to do. It is important to ask for the referral in a way as to not make them feel uncomfortable. Educate them on what an ideal referral is for you.

Take a few minutes to list your top clients: *Clients who you know love you, praise you.*

List 5 - 10 of Your Top Clients

1. _____

2. _____

3. _____

4. _____

5. _____

6. _____

7. _____

8. _____

9. _____

10. _____

Chances are very high that since these are your top clients, these are people who are very ecstatic about you and your services. This is a great start, now all you have to do is ask! Your relationship with these clients will determine how you can ask them. I usually find that a direct approach is the best. I tell them something like, "*I truly appreciate you as a client. I am focusing on growing my business and would like to know if you are comfortable referring me to your friends, family and clients.*" Then, let them know that if they aren't comfortable with this, or wanted time to think about it, that you completely understand and are ok with that as well. Remind them that you value them as a client and thought you would ask for their help.

This way it doesn't put them in an awkward and uncomfortable situation; it gives them an out or gives them an option to help me.

One of the easier referral sources for us to tap into is our friends and family. These are the people who support us in every aspect of our lives, both personally and professionally and they are there for us no matter what. Who better than our loved ones to go to for help to grow our business? They already know and love us! Now, what you do versus what they do depends upon which of your friends and family can potentially refer people to you. In this aspect, it really depends on their understanding of what you do, versus who they know and what they do. That being said, do not prejudge. You never know who might know a potential client or relevant connection and potential referral source for you, so don't even try to guess. This is so important that I am going to say it again... **DO NOT PREJUDGE!**

Now you will make a list of your loved ones who have an understanding of what it is that you do. Regardless of whether you are business to business (B to B) or business to consumer (B to C), and regardless of whether they have a career or not, they still know people. They know people from all aspects of their lives, which is why you can't and shouldn't prejudge. If you do prejudge, this can and will hurt your chances of getting that perfect referral. All you have to do is ask them if they are willing to help you, and then ensure you properly educate them on what it is you do and what you are looking for.

List 5 - 10 of Your Friends and Family

1. _____

2. _____

3. _____

4. _____

5. _____

6. _____

7. _____

8. _____

9. _____

10. _____

Reach out to these people. Don't stop here; if you can come up with more than 10 then by all means do so. The more the merrier. These are people who are the easiest to ask. The more people you are asking who already know you and love you for who you are, the more potential referral sources you are soliciting to help you grow you business. The beauty of this is because they already love you, your success is important to them.

The Casual Referral Source

The next referral source comes from networking. Remember earlier we described networking as any place where you interact with other people. That could be a meeting, a business event, a sports event, church, etc. For the sake of discussing, identifying and establishing referral sources in a networking environment, we will view networking from the perspective of attending events and meetings designed specifically for professional business networking. Similar techniques will be used in other environments, you just need to remember and realize that at other events people may not be there to network, so you must use discretion.

While you are out networking, you are meeting a lot of people. Through this process you want to get to know them. You can do this a lot of ways:

- Doing business with them
- Them doing business with you
- Casual conversation
- Phone conversation
- Meeting in person, possibly over coffee

The sole purpose for doing any or all of the above is to get to know a little bit more about each other. Getting to know each other better, allows you to offer each other a lead, a connection, and sometimes better yet, a referral! Either way, the intention is there to help each other. As the relationship develops, you will find the quality of the referrals will develop as well. Remember, growing business through the development of relationships is not a destination; it is and always will be a journey.

The Strategic Referral Partner

Now that you have finished identifying industry strategic alliances and referral sources as well as how to manage and handle those relationships, let's focus on establishing what the **Perfect Strategic Referral Partner** is for you and your business. *Identify people, businesses, and industries that will service the same client as your business but not compete with you.* This is the mother ship of any and all referral sources you will come across. This is where you want to invest your time. You want to be very clear about this in your head. When you get out there and start networking, these are the people you are going to be seeking.

By strategically aligning yourself with true **Quality Strategic Referral Partners,** the amount of sales representation as well as the strength it offers to your business is amazing. Identifying, establishing and cultivating these types of relationships adds an enormous amount of muscle to your sales force as well as your business.

In order to understand who you are seeking, you need to identify the specific businesses/people/industries that have compatible target markets. Put a lot of thought into this exercise. The more you think outside the box, the more potential industries you will identify as being key for you to pursue future relationships and possible Strategic Referral Partnerships with.

List 5 - 10 Industries which Service the Same Target Market as You but Do Not Compete With Your Business

1. _____

2. _____

3. _____

4. _____

5. _____

6. _____

7. _____

8. _____

9. _____

10. _____

Identifying what makes a good Strategic Referral Partner is key to moving forward. These are the businesses that you will be seeking while you are out networking. Remember, the whole point of networking is to develop relationships. Create a buzz, so to speak. You will be developing a multitude of networking relationships while you are out there, all of which are of extreme value. Some will be casual, others will be intense. The Strategic Referral Partner relationship will be a productively intense relationship as well as one that you will value and cherish for years to come.

Just because you have identified an industry to be key as a potential targeted Strategic Referral Partner does not mean that everybody you run into from this industry will be an ideal Strategic Referral Partner.

It is only through the process of getting to know people and their businesses that you will learn to recognize whether or not they are a perfect fit.

You need to program yourself with the mindset that when you go to networking events that you are going out to:

- Make contacts
- Build relationships
- Add value to other peoples businesses
- Add value to your database through the quality contacts you build relationships with
- Add value to the organizations that you have chosen to join

Most importantly, the #1 mindset shift you need to make is **DO NOT GO OUT WITH THE INTENT TO SELL!** Don't get me wrong, there are times that, by default, just by meeting people you will meet those who will have a want, need or desire to utilize whatever it is that you are selling. But that is not why you are going to networking meetings. This is worth saying again: **Do not show up at a networking meeting with the intent to sell your product, service or idea!**

You are going into networking environments with the sole intent to identify, find, and build relationships with your potential Strategic Referral Partners, as well as with people and businesses that may not be a Strategic Referral Partner but can and will be a referral source. These people are all going to want and need you just as much as you are going to want and need them. You have a significant value to offer each other. This is not going to happen overnight. Relationships take time to cultivate. Trust takes time to build. Fine wines don't age over night, and people don't marry after the first date, so don't expect somebody to open up their database to you the second you tell them what you do and vice versa.

Master Networker Tip #6
After you identify prospective Strategic Referral Partners, do yourself a huge favor... do your DUE DILLIGENCE!

7

The Power of the Strategic Referral Partner

When you build a relationship with a Strategic Referral Partner, the alliance opportunities are endless. Not only is there the potential to be a strong source for referrals, but you can also explore the opportunity of joint marketing ventures together. This could not only save you significant amounts of money but also open up a whole new list of people to whom you can market your product or service to. The beauty is you will have a higher level of credibility to people who you don't know and who don't know you because of the alliance you have with their existing supplier. Since you both have the same type of clientele base, and don't compete against each other, you have essentially doubled your sales force with just this one relationship.

Keep in mind your referral sources and Strategic Referral Partners are not going to go out and sell for you, they are going to be your eyes and ears on the street. They are going to look and listen for opportunities and open doors for you that otherwise you would have never known existed or had no luck opening by yourself in the past. They are going to have the opportunity to make warm introductions for you that make it that much easier for you to get a leg up on your competition. It is very important to keep in mind that this relationship is a partnership, so there are expectations that the relationship will be reciprocated in both directions. It will only work if it is a win-win-win for all concerned. The win-win-win is defined by the relationship being a win for them, a win for you and a win for the potential client. Whether the referred came from your database or theirs, in order for the relationship to be completely successful, the end result has to be a happy and service-satisfied client.

Successful Cycle of a Strategic Referral Partner Relationship

I will share with you two very different personal experiences. I have been a business owner and entrepreneur for over a decade and have built my businesses on networking and relationships. I received a PhD from the school of hard knocks. I learned a lot of my lessons the hard way when it came to networking and building solid relationships with referral sources.

The Tale of the Strategic Referral Partner Nightmare

I found what I thought was an amazing Strategic Referral Partner. It was the perfect scenario. Neither one of our businesses competed at all with the other. We were in the same industry but did not offer the same products. It was because of this that we truly had the capability to be Strategic Referral Partners. I invested a significant amount of time getting to know what it was he did and exactly what he was looking for so I could best communicate his expertise to others when the opportunity presented itself.

The opportunity came up frequently to speak to clients about his products. I was so excited the first time I got to call David and tell him about a meeting I had with one of my clients and that during the course of the conversation I had the opportunity to talk about my new-found Strategic Referral Partner.

Because of the relationship I had with this client, she was also excited that I was recommending him to her. You see, I was saving her and her company so much time and money from having to do their own due diligence in finding a competent representative for their need. It was my relationship with this client that opened the door and rolled out the red carpet for David. Sure enough, days later, the company (David worked for), who I referred to my client, was awarded a very large contract. However, it wasn't David who informed me of this; it was my client who called to thank me for the introduction. Do you see anything wrong with this picture? An important factor in referral relationships of any magnitude is **Communication!** This was something David did very little of during the entire process. I constantly followed up with him to make sure everything was going smoothly and to find out if I could assist in any way. After he secured the order he, at a minimum, should have at least let me know, not to mention possibly thanking me, for referring him to an organization that he may have never met or gotten into for that matter.

Well, for whatever reason, I was so excited about this that I was blinded by the warning signs. I should have known better but I didn't. Months went by, and I kept sending David referral after referral. His company kept winning business because of the doors I was opening for them. Finally, after several months of this one-sided relationship, I called David and asked him why he never returned the favor. Why was it that he had never once referred anyone to me, when in the beginning it was clearly agreed upon that this would be a reciprocal relationship? He claimed that for whatever reason he doesn't seem to run across the opportunities for me as I was for him, but that he would honestly try to work harder on finding something for me. David assured me that I was so valuable to him that he wanted to make sure I was happy. Of course I was valuable to his business, I was their #1 sales producer and I wasn't even on their payroll. He loved me!

Approximately a month after that conversation I got a call from that very first client I had introduced him to, and she was pretty upset with me. My supposed Strategic Referral Partner had dropped the ball on something very large, which was very time sensitive for my client's needs and he was not communicating with her to help her solve this problem. This became an immediate crisis for me, as this was certainly a reflection on me and my business. You are probably thinking it shouldn't have been, but it is. They are doing business together because of an introduction and recommendation I had made. This happened several more times with several of the other referrals I had given to him.

Don't get me wrong, we are all human and businesses have their ups and downs. It isn't as much the fact that **he** dropped the ball that hurt me or the customer, as it was the fact that **he** was avoiding the communication and not trying to go out of **his** way to try to make things right. But I should have known that this type of unprofessionalism and behavior was true to who **he** really was, because all along the relationship was one sided. There was never any reciprocation, no thank you, no acknowledgement, and never any communication. This was not a Strategic Referral Partner. I should have known that after that first "ah ha" moment when my customer was the one who called me to communicate the successful transaction and not **David**. That was my first sign that there was going to be a problem.

Unfortunately, through the course of my professional business networking relationship with David, I had lost a few clients due to him dropping the ball and not communicating with them in a timely manner. If I had done my due diligence a little better in the beginning, by truly spending time getting to know him; how he did business and gotten to know more about his reputation, I would have seen the true David, not the one he wanted me to see. Instead, I eagerly and naively offered up my coveted resources, my clientele, as if they were sacrificial lambs. He unfortunately slaughtered several of these relationships for me because of his lack of professionalism. This was a very expensive lesson for me. I hope you can learn from my mistake and save yourself a lot of grief and financial pain.

Ok, so now that I have scared you with the horror story of the worst case scenario of a Strategic Referral Partnership gone badly, I would like to ease your mind with one that went perfectly by the book and is much more the norm.

Happily Ever After Does Exist
with Strategic Referral Partners

The primary focus of my business, in case you couldn't tell from the previous story, is business to business. So through my networking efforts I came across an insurance agent who was a very dynamic, clean cut down-to-earth kind of guy. His name was Mark. We exchanged cards at a networking meeting and after that neither one of us truly pursued a professional relationship with the other.

After about a month of networking meetings, (and for me that was a lot of meetings because at that time in developing my business I tried to hit several a week), I kept running into him at almost every meeting. I think I was seeing Mark more than my family. Our networking relationship was very casual at this point. We had exchanged casual conversations and pleasantries. We understood a little bit about each other's businesses, but for whatever reason, the connection had never triggered any further pursuance of a deeper professional networking relationship. After continually running into each other, we decided we needed to meet for coffee and get to know each other a little more, so we did. It was the best thing both of us could have done for our businesses. We met for only about an hour or so at a local coffee shop. We each spent an equal amount of time discussing what we do and what our ideal client looks like. Through the course of talking with each other we realized we really had the same focus and that our target markets were almost identical.

A few days later one of my favorite clients had an insurance problem, it was a pretty big issue for them, and they weren't having any luck getting it resolved with their insurance company. She didn't know what to do so I called Mark and he told her exactly what to do to get her situation handled. It was amazing; I looked like a hero in her eyes and so did he.

Months went by and she called me for his information because her company's insurance was up for renewal and she wanted to give Mark an opportunity to submit a quote. Sure enough, he landed the largest contract he had ever signed in his career.

Throughout all the months and years we have known each other; we have had a very strong reciprocal referral relationship. I can't tell you the amount of business we exchanged in referrals, but it has been very significant. We each had a salesperson representing us on the street; an ally, a friend, a trustworthy source that wasn't on payroll, didn't receive compensation, and would willingly communicate our capabilities to anyone we ran into. That, my friend, is a **TRUE STRATEGIC REFERRAL PARTNER!!!**

The Anatomy of the Perfect Strategic Referral Partner

Being a Strategic Referral Partner comes with a lot of responsibilities. A few, but not all, of these responsibilities are:

- Referral Representation
- Strategic Introductions
- Exchange of Information

You need to identify who could potentially be a good Strategic Referral Partner for you. Yes, I know this is very similar to the exercise I had you do in Chapter 5. Indulge me. It's alright if some of your answers are the same.

Here are a few examples to help trigger some thought.

Example 1

Let's say you are a massage therapist. Your focus for the most part is B2C (Business to Consumer). In some cases you may have a B2B focus, but for this example we will focus on B2C. Your more obvious target Strategic Referral Partners could be an acupuncturist, a chiropractor, a personal trainer and a gym owner. Your less obvious, or as I like to refer to them your 'outside the box,' potential Strategic Referral Partners' could be a hairstylist, a manicurist, an esthetician, a photographer, a health insurance agent, a personal liability insurance agent, a life coach and a residential real estate agent. A short list, all of which for the most part, focus on B2C as well as have a target market with disposable income.

Example 2

Let's say you own or sell for a printing company. Your focus for the most part is B2B (Business to Business). Your more obvious Strategic Referral Partners could be a promotional products company, a sign manufacturer, a CD/DVD duplicating company and a silk screener. Potentially less obvious partners might be a commercial banker, a commercial lender, a commercial real estate agent, a business insurance agent, a telecommunications company, a copier sales company, and a copywriter / editor, to name a few.

I hope these examples got your creative juices flowing. So take a few minutes to make a list of industries that focus on the same market as you do which do not compete with your business.

Potential Strategic Referral Partner Industry List

1. _____

2. _____

3. _____

4. _____

5. _____

Now that you have identified who you are looking for, identify what you can and cannot truly offer to them. Be honest with yourself and remember you can't be everything to everybody.

In Chapter 4, I asked you to identify your strengths. Whether your strengths are product related, service related or the moral foundation of what your business was built on, pick your top two or three from that list. These strengths are what you are going to use to deliver your message to the market, as well as teach others to deliver the message for you. We will get into this more in the next chapter as well as later on in the book. I just want you to make note of what they are now.

Please save yourself some heartache and don't put, high level of service or anything to do with service for that matter, in your top three. I promise you that that is the same thing your competitor is touting.

Top 3 Business Strengths

1. _____

2. _____

3. _____

You have an understanding of what is important to you, the type of person and business that is beneficial for you to align yourself and your business with. All of this is going to serve you well and be very beneficial toward you in your journey to seeking the Perfect Strategic Referral Partner.

The stronger your relationships are with your Strategic Referral Partners the more in depth you will be able to get with them regarding everything about your business. Don't be afraid to share with them your weaknesses, as they may have ideas to help you that may have never occurred to you. They also may be able to offer masterminding and brainstorming sessions, which will benefit both of you and your businesses moving forward. Two brains are always better than one and sometimes we are too close to things to see what is so obvious. As I stated earlier, the opportunities with Strategic Referral Partners are endless.

Master Networker Tip #7
Be very creative in all the ways that you
and a Strategic Referral Partner
can work together in helping
each other build businesses.
Don't let FEAR keep you from
Thinking Outside the Box.'

8

The Strategic Referral Partner and Management System (SRPM)

There is a lot of merit to the old adage "If You Fail to Plan, You Plan to Fail." SRPM is very important to your networking success. The whole point of networking is to identify, interview and partner with quality, like-minded people. The key words here are *quality* and *like-minded*. This is where so many people fail. They run to networking meetings, bring their business cards, brochures and other marketing materials, and shove them in everybody's faces selling their product, service or solution. They go out of their way to netSELL and netVOMIT all over people. For them, it is about quantity and not quality. It is very hard to build a relationship with people like this. They network strictly to make a transaction and rarely a connection. There is a huge difference between hunting and farming.

Let's put that in another perspective many of us can appreciate. Ladies, do you want to go out on a first date and get pregnant? Men, do you want to find out the next day that you're bound to this person for life that you barely know? I don't know about you, but I really don't want to get pregnant on the first date. I would really like to court, be courted, and by all means, definitely get to know you first. How is that for an analogy?

Keep this analogy in mind as you go out there networking and connecting from this point forward. Occasionally you will meet someone that has a want, need or desire for your product, service or solution. But realistically your intent is to put yourself out there to make connections, sift and sort those connections, and then work on the relationship. It is necessary and important for each of you to get to know each other's businesses, personalities, professionalism level, target markets, and principles that you each built your businesses on. This will help you effortlessly refer to them and vice versa.

Don't confuse a Strategic Referral Partner strictly as a Word of Mouth Marketing (WOMM)/referral source. Don't get me wrong, WOMM/referrals are part of your strategic partner's responsibilities; however it's not their only responsibility. WOMM/referrals will happen organically the more you are out there networking and spreading the word about your business.

Please keep in mind that WOMM is not always positive. The way you "show up" and represent your business and your integrity will determine whether WOMM turns out to be positive or negative. And trust me when I tell you negative WOMM is much more viral than its positive WOMM cousin. Positive WOMM and referrals will happen through connections you make networking regardless if somebody is a Strategic Referral Partner or not. They are not as frequent and usually not as qualified as a referral, but they do happen.

SRPM is very important moving forward. You must be very clear in your mind, as well as willing and capable of communicating these expectations to your potential Strategic Referral Partners.

- How do you want this relationship to be?
- What are some of your expectations?
- What it is you have to offer to their business?
- How you are going to educate them about who you are and what you do?
- Be clear on the amount of time you have to offer them in reciprocation.
- Yes it is a two way street!

So let's start with expectations. Remember going into this, whatever you expect from your referral sources you must be willing and able to return to them. So there are a couple of key points to consider before putting together a list of potential expectations. Knowing that you are responsible for fulfilling the same obligations as you are expecting from Strategic Referral Partners, it is key to identify how many Strategic Referral Partners you are going to initially seek out. Time management must be an issue because if you are not careful you could potentially fail in multiple aspects. So I would start out slowly and try not to be overzealous in the beginning. As your Strategic Referral Partner relationships mature they become second nature and less time consuming so it becomes easier to take on more. Take them on slowly and in moderation in the beginning. You will be doing yourself, your client and your Strategic Referral Partners a huge favor.

The best way to figure out what your expectations of a Strategic Referral Partner will be is to identify what it is you are willing and capable of doing for them. The options are endless. Your relationship with each referral partner will be different, and that is ok as long as it is mutually beneficial and takes you both down the path to achieving your desired goals. Here are just a few suggestions to consider, but be creative and open to pursuing other ideas as well:

- Understand each other's business enough to be able to best communicate it to others.
- Co-op marketing ventures together:
  - Postcards
  - Advertisements
  - Flyers
  - Handouts
  - Trade shows and expos
- Continually look for opportunities to offer each other's products and services.
- Offer joint promotions/package offers and discount offerings then market them within each other's databases.
- Brainstorming and masterminding.
- Create joint educational webinars/seminars to educate your prospects/clients about how your product or service, together with your Strategic Referral Partner's product or service, can best solve their problem.

- Schedule a Strategic Referral Partner ride-along day
  - ✓ This is where each of you schedule appointments with key clients and take your Strategic Referral Partner along with you to meet and edify them.
  - ✓ This is a great strategy to help open key doors for each other. But don't sabotage your client and surprise them with a guest. Make sure it is clear you are bringing somebody who you really want them to meet.

There are so many other creative things you can do together to help support each other. Don't limit yourself to the above list; use it only as a reference to stimulate your brain into thinking of many other creative ways you and a Strategic Referral Partner can work together. You just need to understand your needs, understand their needs and understand the time and effort you each have to offer the relationship.

Characteristics of Your Strategic Partner

The next thing you are going to want to consider is what characteristics are appealing to you in a Strategic Referral Partner. You see, not just anybody can fit this role. They have to be ideal for you and bring a lot to the table. So you need to consider what type of relationship can bring you the biggest bang for your buck. Your buck in this case is your time, your energy, your reputation, and your most coveted asset of all, your clientele. In order to make this investment, you want to get a very large return. Be choosey; you deserve to be. You have worked very hard for all of the above mentioned assets and have every right to want a return on your investment.

Consider what the ideal Strategic Referral Partner would be for your business. If your focus is Business to Business (B2B) key characteristics could include:

- Size of the company
- Their database
- Profession
- Industry
- Reputation
- Annual revenue
- Sales presence
- Key clients
- Duration – time in business

If your focus is Business to Consumer (B2C), then your considerations could be very similar and you may want to look at:

- Complimentary product offering
- Large clientele and following
- Reputation
- Quality
- Pricing
- Services
- Compatibility of their product offering in comparison to yours

So many different scenarios play a large part in deciding what the ideal Strategic Referral Partner will be for you and your business.

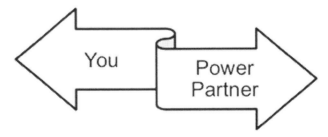

The next thing you want to take a look at is what you have to offer to a Strategic Referral Partner. This is pretty important moving forward with SPPM. Remember, this is a two way street. You are interested in establishing a Strategic Referral Partnership with somebody because of what you each can bring to the table for each other and your businesses. Although each of your businesses move in different directions, there are enough similarities to connect the two of you and because of this you are somewhat attached.

In order for it to be a partnership, there needs to be something in it for both of you. So it's time to go back to what your strengths are that you identified earlier in Chapter 4.

- Are your gross receipts attractive to this perspective partner?
- How about your clientele?
- Is there anybody in your database who is just going to wow them?
- Do you have a significant number of strong relationships that can be of value to this perspective partner?
- How about "feet on the street"? Is your sales team of value to them or are you just a one person show?

There is nothing wrong with being a one person show; you just need to keep things in perspective and not over commit or over promise.

Are you bringing as much to the table initially as what has attracted you to them?

Educating Your Strategic Partner

You have now identified what it is that you want to get out of a Strategic Referral Partnership and what you have to put into one. You now need to figure out how you are going to educate a Strategic Referral Partner to talk about you and communicate your business to others in order to pique their interest enough to want to meet with you. Sounds easy enough doesn't it? Well not really. You see, you are the "expert" and your knowledge about your business can truly bog somebody down to the point of confusion. *People don't really care about all the technical nuances of what it is we offer. They want to know the sexy basics.*

You can't expect your Strategic Referral Partners to know everything about what it is you do, especially in the beginning of a newly developing relationship. They have their own business to manage. You need to educate them just enough about your business to get the referral relationship started. Remember, they are just opening doors for you. It is not their responsibility to close business for you. However, in some cases this could potentially happen just by default, depending upon what it is you offer, your price point and their relationship with the client.

This is where some of the work you did in Chapter 4 and Chapter 5 is really going to help you. Knowing and understanding you and your business is very essential here and will help you concisely communicate your capabilities and what it is you are seeking in a referral partnership.

Communicating and educating what it is you do is very key to growing and developing business with or without a Strategic Referral Partner. You know what you say to prospective clients when you meet with them:

• Why they should do business with you
• What you offer
• Your capabilities
• Things that differentiate you from the competition

Well, all of that does your Strategic Referral Partner no good. It is too much information and frankly, pitching your business is your responsibility not theirs. Take all of the above mentioned information and condense it down to a 1-3 minute presentation. This is a little more than an elevator speech but a lot less than your prospective client presentation. It must be easily duplicated and it must highlight who and what you offer to pique somebody to open the door for the next phase, and that is you having the opportunity to present to them why you are a solution for them.

Referral Worksheet

Ideal Prospects/Referral and Clients

- Air/Heat Repair (5 or more trucks)
- Plumbers (5 or more vehicles)
- Electricians (5 or more vehicles)
- Auto Repair
- Manufacturers
- Distributors
- Hospitals
- Medical Offices (3 or more Drs.)
- High End Day Spas
- Realtors (who want to differentiate themselves)
- Recovery Homes
- Non Profits
- Sports Organizations
- Schools

What to Look For

- Letterhead
- Envelopes
- Business Cards
- Business Forms/NCR
- Brochures
- Flyers
- Postcards
- Presentation Folders
- Note Pads
- Manuals
- Directories
- Catalogs
- Magazines

Referral Worksheet

Power Partners

- CPA/Bookkeepers
- Web Designers
- Business Insurance
- Business Attorneys
- Business Bankers
- Payroll Companies
- Business Caterers
- HR Companies
- Non Profits

What to Listen For

- I need to work on branding my company
- I need a logo
- I spend too much money on postage
- My printer went out of business
- I just did a photo shoot
- I can't get my artwork from...
- I need to save money
- I need more money
- I need more customers
- I need to differentiate myself from my competition
- I did a mailing once and it didn't work

How you educate your Strategic Referral Partner on your target market and what it is you are looking for is very important. You want it to be easy for them to understand and communicate. Don't overwhelm them or bog them down. I know this is going to be hard to believe but despite how amazing your business is, you are not a solution for everybody. Trust me when I tell you I was personally heartbroken when I figured that out. I thought everybody needed me and my services. OK, you can stop laughing now.

Luckily, most Strategic Referral Partners have similar target markets, so the fact that you both go after the same prospects helps a lot because they already have an understanding of the type of client you are seeking. You still need to get specific in communicating to them who your target market truly is and really drill down to the specifics of your ideal client, your perfect referral. **You need to help them help you. In order for them to be able to help you,** it has to be easy. *Remember, they have their own business to develop and manage.*

You have to *remember* they are out selling themselves, networking, building relationships, and generating activity for their own business. You are somewhere in the back of their mind. They need buzz words, lingo, they need to know what keywords they are listening for to help introduce you to the people they are meeting. What is it that they can potentially hear somebody say that will move you from the back of their brain to the front of their brain in a matter of seconds? This is what you want to focus on with them.

To best help educate my Referral Partners, both Casual and Strategic, I designed a Referral Worksheet. This Referral Worksheet helped me stay on track while we were meeting, so I could ensure that I was best educating them to help refer to me as well as to make sure I didn't forget anything. This really streamlined our initial "getting to know" each other process. The Referral Worksheet was also a great tool for my Referral Partners, because they could take it with them. The easier you make it for someone to refer to you, the more frequently they will refer to you. I keep a binder of all my Strategic Power Partners Referral Worksheets. This way I can ensure that I stay abreast of their needs, wants and desires. When we meet, I will bring it with me so I can note any changes they may have in their business needs.

Your Role in SRPM

Now that we have been through everything you could possibly want, need and desire from a Strategic Referral Partner, it is now time to discuss **the #1 important responsibility** in the SRPM. That is **YOUR ROLE!** Now that you have identified what is significant for your business and have a Strategic Referral Partner, you need to realize that it is important for you to learn as much about your referral partner's business. You also need to be able to successfully communicate and represent them and help open doors for their ideal clients and prospects. This means not only assuming all of the responsibilities associated with being a Strategic Referral Partner, but also going into this knowing you are the one that has to take the lead.

When you meet someone, lead with the knowledge that you are there to serve them, help them, and get to know them.

- What is it that you are willing to do?
- What is it that you are capable of doing?
- How much time do you have to offer this relationship?

The most important part of a networking relationship of any magnitude is what you can, will and are doing for them!!! Each SRPM will be unique to each individual relationship.

This will ultimately be the beginning of a strong networking relationship. Regardless of whether or not the person becomes a Strategic Referral Partner, they will still become a reciprocal referral source. It is extremely important to identify how much time you have in your business to invest in establishing this unique referral relationship. This is why I mentioned earlier to take the pursuance of Strategic Referral Partners slowly in the beginning. It truly is an investment of time, and as the relationship progresses the time needed to invest becomes less, which will then allow you to take on another partner, and then another, and so on.

Managing Your Networking Efforts

Outside of running your business, how much time do you have left to network / market your business? You need to identify how much time each week you have to invest in networking as a marketing and advertising concept. This is an important piece of your puzzle, because time management is very crucial to successful networking and relationship building. If you are not careful with managing your time, networking can take on a life of it's own. This in some cases is not a bad thing; remember, people do business with people they know, like and trust. That being said, the more you need to work in your business versus on your business, time management is of the essence so that you can actually do business. We will get into a networking plan in a few chapters, to help you ensure you are leveraging your time to the fullest extent.

What you are trying to come up with right now is how many hours you have to dedicate to networking. Networking is a multiple-tiered process which consists of:

- Investing time going to events, meetings and mixers
- The time you spend on follow up calls
- The one-on-one time you spend with fellow networkers and Strategic Referral Partners

In the beginning of the Strategic Referral Partner establishment and relationship it is safe to say you will want to allocate a couple hours a month, possibly more, to each Strategic Referral Partner. This does not include the time you are at networking meetings, that is additional connecting and farming time. Every second you spend with a Strategic Referral Partner is an investment. After the relationship is established and you are both referring machines for the other, you will find that the duration spent together decreases but the frequency you see each other increases. What I mean by that is you will spend less time together when you are together, except lunches, social events and the like, but you will find yourself communicating with your Strategic Referral Partner more frequently on the phone, or quick meetings or drive-bys, etc. This is why you will be able to add Strategic Referral Partners as your relationships progress.

Master Networker Tip #8
Help Referral Sources and Power Partners help you and ensure that they help you help them.

9

Center of Influence

What does Center of Influence possibly have to do with you going to networking meetings? How about **EVERYTHING!!!!** You see, it's all about what you bring to the table, what you have to offer people you are out connecting with at meetings. You are going to network with the frame of mind to be of service to others. You are not dialing into the traditional radio station **WIIFM (What's In It For Me)**. You are going digital: you are dialing into **WIIFT (What's In It For Them)**. This is why **WHO** you know and **HOW** well you know them is so IMPORTANT. The sooner you completely understand your database and your level of influence within it, connecting needs, wants and desires with products, services and solutions becomes second nature to you, and the more successful networking will become for you.

Determining Your Center of Influence

Depending on how organized you are as a sales/business person will determine how easy this next task will be for you. You will want to get out your database, both personal and professional. It's time to open up either your CRM (Customer Relationship Management) program or your little black book, or a combination of your Smartphone, Rolodex, social media pages, Outlook, PDA, Post-It notes, stack of business cards, accounting program, invoice history and whatever else you have managed to use to scatter all of your contact information.

While you are going through your contacts and re-familiarizing yourself with everybody you know; I want you to review everybody from a different perspective than usual. This is going to be easier for some of the people you know than others. That's ok. All you are trying to identify is the influence you have in these relationships.

- What type of role do you play in their life?
- What type of role do you play in their business?
- What is your level of influence with them?
- What role do they hold professionally and personally?
- What are their likes and dislikes?
- What are their hobbies?

Identifying who they are professionally, as well as who are they personally, and the role you play in their life/business, is doubly important both in your value as a referral source and your value as a connection source.

Imagine being in a position that whenever your client, prospective client, referral partner or Strategic Referral Partner needs something or anything, regardless of whether or not you offer it, you are the person who comes to mind for them to call. This is because you have managed to identify yourself as a person of influence, the person who knows everybody and not just anybody, but people of high quality. This is a very powerful, influential position to hold. This is another important factor to successful networking, the value you bring to the relationship.

Regardless of what side you sit on, if you make a successful connection you are a hero. The key word there is a successful connection. You don't just want to be the "Google" of connections; the internet exists for that sole purpose. You are adding value when you connect, recommend and refer.

Rules of Referability

Put some parameters on connections and referrals that you are willing to make. I will share with you the rule of thumb I live by to determine whether or not somebody is of the caliber for me to refer them.

Rule #1
Would I use them?

Followed closely by...

Rule #2
Would I refer them to my mother?

There are a lot of criteria involved in answering both of those questions. Such as:

- Do I know somebody who has recently used them?
- What is the feedback / experience?
- How long have I known them?
- Do I know them well enough to let them into my inner circle?

You don't want to refer somebody who may not service your referrals properly. You are staking part of your reputation on offering this referral. Understand that the person you gave the referral to has ownership in making the decision whether or not to use the person you referred, but I have found in some cases someone will use somebody's product or service just because of my recommendation.

The two cardinal rules of thumb I live by work the same in reverse. You do not want to refer somebody who will not follow through with full integrity, such as not paying for the product or service, or being such high maintenance that doing business with them is hardly worth the money. If I know up front that somebody is a high maintenance referral, I will warn the person I am referring them to before I ever make the connection. That type of information is extremely appreciated. Trust me, they will thank you for the warning. So I use similar rules in connecting a need with a solution.

Rule #1
Would I sell to them?

Followed closely by ...

Rule #2
Would I ask my mother to sell to them?

When looking for referrals and organizing your database, focus on your inner circle; this primarily is where you hold a fair amount of influence. Identify your:

- Family
- Friends
- Employees / co-workers
- Neighbors
- Key customers

This should give you a decent core of people who you have a fair amount of influence with so as you are meeting people you have a Center of Influence that may have a want, need or desire. When you find yourself out there, and you identify quality business people who offer a quality product or service, you can quickly go through your organized database and identify where there might be a need and you can start connecting needs with solutions.

Here are a couple examples. I went to a networking meeting a few weeks ago. I was new to this group, and I only knew a couple of people who belonged to this organization. I diligently listened to the commercials, connected with several people before and after the meeting, and left. A few days went by, and I got an email from a friend of mine asking me if I knew a business attorney who did trademarks and copyrights. My brain started going through its database and I recalled meeting a business attorney in this group. So I called someone that I did know in the group and asked her opinion of this attorney because I didn't have any personal experience with her yet, and I haven't known her long enough to have formed my own opinion. My friend had spoken very highly of this attorney and said she could easily recommended and refer her to anyone. So I called the attorney, who I barely knew, and told her what my friend was looking for and made the connection. I'm not sure if anything will ever come out of it for either of them; however, they both appreciated the fact that I thought enough of them to make the connection. I am meeting with the attorney this coming week so we can better understand what each other does. As I stated earlier, my primary focus is business to business. I look forward to growing a mutually beneficial relationship and I now know somebody else in this networking group, so my warm reception has gone from two to three.

To give you another example, I was sitting in a client's office that I had been doing business with for about six months. They were redoing all of their marketing collateral and through casual conversation she was explaining to me how burdened she has been trying to write and put together all the copy for their website and other marketing materials. This was taking up so much of her time and unfortunately there were other things that were more pressing and their new marketing launch kept getting delayed. I told her that I knew an amazing professional writer who specialized in doing exactly what it was that she didn't have time to take care of herself. She asked me how somebody outside the company could possibly do justice to writing about their product. I laughed and shrugged my shoulders and said, "I don't know, that's her profession not mine. I just know she has done work for several people I know and they have all highly recommended her." She agreed it was worth a try. I connected the two of them the very next day and within a few weeks, their project was complete. Everybody was happy! I had a happy client and the person I gave the referral to was happy because she had a nice payday and you know what, they were both happy with me. So happy in fact, the reciprocation was amazing. I ended up growing that account over 150% in a year-to-year comparison, and the professional writer, referred a few new clients to me. This was a win-win-win.

By now I am hoping you see the importance of your database and understanding the level of influence you carry with each person. Protect your contacts, share them sparingly, and make sure that when you do make a connection, it is a win-win for all involved. I know what you're probably thinking right now: *I don't know that many people; I haven't been networking that long, so I don't have a lot of referral sources, and my family and friends are tired of being sold to all the time.* Trust me when I tell you that the more you put yourself out there going to networking meetings, events and mixers, the larger your database will become and your Center of Influence will grow. This will open up many more opportunities for you to offer valuable connections and you will become a more influential networker. This takes time; it doesn't happen overnight. There is definitely some validity in the saying that your social worth is a direct reflection of your net worth. Your database is your **Gold Mine**; you have every right to take care of them.

While you are building your Center of Influence you want to look for other Centers of Influence. This concept can be utilized strategically. If you are new to an event, meeting or organization, seeking out the Centers of Influence in the room will help you meet people quickly.

Centers of Influence will easily be spotted. This is the person who is surrounded by people. This Influencer could be the president of the organization, someone who holds a leadership position or somebody who is a Master Networker, and because of this, people want to be around the Center of Influencer (COI). The COI has a significant amount of influence within the group. Seeking them out and getting to know them can benefit you in multiple ways. A COI is definitely the type of person you want to surround yourself with, as well as strive to become yourself.

Very important rule to remember about Centers of Influencers, they are very seasoned. You must be willing and able to build authentic and mutually beneficial relationships. Trust will not be given, it must be earned. Make the investment and it will pay you dearly, mess up and it will cost you dearly.

Master Networker Tip #9

Know your Center of Influence,
seek out Centers of Influencers
and become known as a
Center of Influence.

10

Developing Your Commercial

As a salesperson/networker, (yes, regardless of whether you are an entrepreneur, business owner or employee, you fit into both of these categories) there are a lot of different types of presentations you will find yourself having to be prepared to give. We are going to focus on three primary commercials that you will be called upon to do while you network.

1. The Meet and Greet – a.k.a. The Elevator Speech
2. The 30 – 60 second Commercial
3. The 10 – 20 minute Presentation

Although these commercials are similar, they are actually very different. It is important to be prepared to deliver these commercials when you go out networking. The type of event you are attending will determine which of these commercials you will deliver and in some cases it will be all of them. Some events allow you to deliver a 30 – 60 second commercial. Others are structured for meet and greet during open floor networking. There are other events where you have the opportunity to do both. Then there are meetings where a few times a year, you will have the opportunity to highlight your business for 10-20 minutes.

A typical networking meeting is structured something like this:

• Open floor networking
• Member and guest commercial spots
• Miscellaneous agenda items
• Possibly a guest speaker
• Open floor networking

Meet and Greet

Open floor networking is a significant part of a networking meeting. This particular meeting structure gives you time to do a lot of meet and greet. This is not the time to chat about the family, or weekend, or kids, or anything unrelated to business and making connections. Remember, you are on a mission. This is the time to be doing exactly what it is called "meet and greet". This is crucial working and connecting time. You are looking for quality people to align yourself with for a potential future business connection and alliance. Your job is to sift and sort. During the meet and greet you will be identifying potential casual referral sources vs. potential strategic referral sources. You will not have the time to "get to know" people during this time, it is just meant to be an initial introduction. Don't get me wrong, if you frequently attend the same meeting, you will by default get to know people and be social with them. Networking is a very social approach to marketing and advertising, so because of this, socializing will happen. It's just not the purpose of this connecting time.

Before the meeting starts, you want to meet as many people as possible. In order to do this, you have to be effective with the delivery of who you are and what you do. Remember, networking is a two way street, so as much as we need to focus on connections, connecting and adding value to relationships, we also have to ensure it is reciprocated and that we allow the other party to share with us who they are and what they do. One of the tools to assist in that is being very clear on who we are and what we do. This will streamline the time you have to invest in networking so that you will have the opportunity to meet more people and find prospective Strategic Referral Partners and Referral Sources.

Because you are there to serve, reciprocate and be a networking and referral machine, it is always good to remember another very important tip. **You have two ears and one mouth; that means you should listen twice as much as you speak!**

For efficiency purposes you should target *3–5 minutes per person* during the meet and greet session of a meeting. There will be some people you will spend less time with and others' maybe a little more, but it is a safe benchmark. So dividing that time in half gives us 1.5–2.5 minutes to tell somebody about your business. It has taken you a lifetime to become an expert in your profession. You can talk about it forever because you have so much passion for your business. *That is why you have to be prepared and know how to explain who you are and what you do!*

How do you educate your fellow networkers on what you do, or who you are seeking, and what a good referral is for you? The answer is simple. Educate through a strategically developed, clearly communicated commercial. You need to have a variety of 30 – 60 second commercials created so that when you are asked what it is YOU do; you are clear, concise and to the point. There are so many thoughts and opinions about what makes the perfect recipe, as well as the different circumstances as to when they should be utilized.

In a meet and greet scenario, some prefer to use the following formula:

- Your name
- Your company name
- A brief description of your company's products/services.

While others prefer using the **WOW Factor**,

- Tell them your name
- A catchy, vague statement to engage them describing the solution your business offers.
- This technique has them asking you questions. It has them unsure as to what it is you do so they want to know more. This style of engagement could intrigue them or frustrate them, so be careful.

As for my opinion regarding the meet and greet commercial, it's pretty simple. It's all about **AUTHENTICITY**. Remember, networking is a people business. If you are not being authentic then you will not be comfortable. If you are not comfortable, then the people you are conversing with feel your discomfort and will be uncomfortable as well. It is important to be comfortable and confident with your delivery and ensure you communicate the essential information, regardless of your delivery, whether you use the standard or the WOW factor meet and greet style. You want to ensure that you get the point across about who you are and what you do. Deliver your meet and greet commercial however it is most congruent to who you are, and this will ensure the highest level of authenticity. It is important to remember you both have a lot of other people to meet, so the key to effective connecting is congruency, authenticity while maintaining complete transparency, and remember to keep it efficient because time is of the essence.

30 – 60 Second Commercial

Another opportunity you may have to give another type of commercial is typically during the meeting when there are member and guest introductions. The anatomy of this commercial is much different. All eyes in the room are focused on you; you should have their complete attention. What are you going to say? This is where you need to think of the commercial industry **POWER PLAYERS**; what do they do? You see it and hear it every day. They spend hundreds of thousands, sometimes millions, of dollars on radio and TV to educate their audience, their consumers and their prospects. Take your cue from them; this is your time to shine. You are the expert, let everyone know it. You will have anywhere from 30 to 60 seconds to educate, inform and perform. Sitting in this room are potentially some of your best potential future referral sources, your future sales team so to speak. It is very important to educate them on what a good referral is for you. **DO NOT** be afraid to give them a company name and/or person's name that you would like to meet. You never know if your ideal dream client has a friend, relative, spouse or neighbor sitting in this room. BE SPECIFIC! To make this count, and in order to really get a bang for your buck, you really want to be prepared so you can "**Educate**" them on:

- Who you are
- What you do
- What a good referral is for you
- What you are looking for (be specific)
- What they can look for to help you
- Then leave them with an amazing tag line

You want to **Communicate, Educate and Motivate** so they will want to find you after the meeting to exchange information for a follow-up meeting so you can get to know each other more.

It is important that you have this commercial prepared so that when you are called upon, you can stand up and deliver it with prepared confidence and not fumble for words or stumble through your opportunity. Take advantage of this time to shine. The biggest injustice you can do to yourself is to attempt to prepare your commercial while others are delivering their commercials.

This is **extremely** valuable time for you for two reasons:

1. It is your responsibility as a fellow networker to listen to the commercials
   a. To identify if there is anybody you can help
   b. To identify whether they have a service that could help one of your contacts
   c. To identify who else you need to connect with after the meeting
2. Most importantly, to ensure your commercial has a strategic relevance
   a. When we just throw something out there it may or may not stick.

However, if we have a solid commercial strategy, whether it's a quarterly strategy, semi-annual or an annual strategy to implement, you are way ahead of the game. When you see commercials on TV, they just don't talk about whatever. The big corporations know exactly what their message is, why they are delivering that particular message and when they are going to deliver it. Do you put this much planning into the delivery of your commercial? If not, why? It works for them, why wouldn't you model your behavior after a successful one?

If the meeting is fairly large in size it won't be possible to connect with everybody during the initial meet and greet before the meeting starts. This is why it is imperative that you keep your radar on for who and what you are looking to connect with and the only way to do that is to PAY ATTENTION to others' commercials. They exist so you can educate others and they can educate you. If you are busy formulating your commercial, trying to figure out what you are going to say, then you will miss a golden opportunity to fill a potential want, need or desire in your database with a potential product, service or solution. Develop a strategic pool of commercials to pick from at any given time, so you will always be prepared.

Master Networker Tip #10
Ensure while developing and delivering your commercials that you are very specific about who and what your are looking for. Eliminate the words "Anybody, Somebody and Everybody" from your vocabulary.

11

Finding the Right Groups and Organizations

Finding the right organizations to focus your networking efforts on is a key element to how successful you will be in networking. This is a task you don't want to take lightly. You not only have a financial outlay attached to joining an organization and participating in its events but you also have the most valuable commodity of all at stake: your time. So you need to make these choices wisely. Yes I said choices. You want to ensure that you diversify your networking approach and join different types of organizations. In most cases you're not going to want to be a one trick pony. There are multiple reasons as to why you are going to join more than one.

Reasons for Joining Multiple Organizations

- Increases opportunity of meeting quality networkers
- Increases database and potential Centers of Influence
- Diversifies the types of people you will meet
- The more you are seen, the more your credibility increases

When we did the Understanding your Business exercise in Chapter 5, understanding what you have to offer, what your industry has to offer, and what the perceptions are of your industry, are all very helpful tools while you are looking for the right organizations. Diversifying your attention and your memberships is another reason why you need to know the information you gained from that exercise. Your business, its prospects, target market and capabilities are very relevant to your networking efforts.

Determine Your Networking Area

If you have a business that people have to commute to in order to receive your services, then you need to keep this in mind when identifying a radius appropriate for networking. In other words, if you offer a service-related business such as car repair, massage, dental, chiropractic, etc., there is a strong probability that people may not want to drive a significant distance to receive your services. I didn't say that they wouldn't, I am just saying that they probably wouldn't. You want to keep this in mind when picking your networking circumference. So it is important to determine your networking area taking into consideration a circumference relevant to your ability to service and attract. This can be as small as a few miles, or as many as 20 miles, or in some cases even further. This solely depends on your business and industry. You may have a general idea of the commutability of your business and industry, or you may want to do some research to help you determine the average distance people are willing to travel for your particular product/service.

Once you have a focal area for networking, you need to identify the different types of networking environments available in that area. Notice I didn't say different networking *organizations*, I said networking *environments*. There are many different types of Networking Groups. Each group serves a specific purpose. I will briefly mention a few:

- Closed Networking Groups
- Open Networking Groups
- Miscellaneous Networking Opportunities

Closed Networking Groups

This type of group typically meets weekly and each member is expected to attend every meeting and has a more strict attendance policy than other types of networking environments. A Closed Networking Group may also be known as a category-specific or category-exclusive networking group. One seat gets reserved for each profession. This will block out your competition from joining the group.

During a Closed Networking Meeting each member has an opportunity to briefly tell the others about their business and what a good referral is for them. Members also have the opportunity to make a presentation to explain their business in more detail, typically for five to ten minutes. This schedule will rotate weekly between the members. Group leaders may provide some training on networking skills or business development and, of course, members pass leads or referrals. This format ensures that each member has a good understanding of the other members' businesses. Typically each member takes an oath to become a "virtual salesperson" so to speak, for the members of the group.

Most Closed Networking Groups encourage visitors to attend their meetings to see if the group would be a good fit for their business and vice versa. Visitors are able to attend two or three meetings before they are required to join. If the group already has a member in the same business, the visitor may then be referred to another chapter within the organization where their profession is not represented.

There are three industry leaders in the category exclusive environment: BNI, LeTip and TEAM Referral Network. All three are very good at what they do and all three offer similar but different benefits. Do your research to determine which organization best aligns with you. *Then you will want to dig deeper and do your due diligence because each chapter within the organizations carries their own dynamics. Just because you align with an organization, does not mean you will align with every chapter within that organization.*

Take a moment to list a few Closed Networking Groups that may be of interest to you that are within the circumference you have chosen.

Closed Groups of Interest

1. _____

2. _____

3. _____

4. _____

5. _____

Open Networking Groups

Open Networking Groups such as Chambers of Commerce and business associations are open to anyone who wants to join. This means that there can be several members of the same profession in the organization. Most of these groups are organized to promote business within a specific geographical area or demographic.

Open Networking Groups tend to be less formally structured than the Closed Networking Groups. Many groups meet after business hours, where one member hosts the meeting at their place of business and members have the opportunity to network as well as see another member's business. An Open Networking Group may also have business meetings and lead-sharing meetings with a format similar to the meetings of Closed Networking Groups.

Chamber of Commerces generally address local political issues and support the communities they represent. It is generally a good idea to join the Chamber where your business is located.

To get the most from an Open Networking Group, regular attendance at meetings is important. The more you are seen, the more you are remembered. The format and structure of these meetings typically offer a limited opportunity for each member to explain his or her business to all the other members during the meeting. It's very important that the members take the responsibility for meeting other members and learning about each others' businesses. On the other hand, the less-structured format of a business meeting after hours allows members to spend extra time with each other.

Take a moment to list a few Open Networking Groups that may be of interest to you that are within the circumference you have chosen.

Open Groups of Interest

1. _____

2. _____

3. _____

4. _____

5. _____

Miscellaneous Networking Opportunities

Not all networking opportunities present themselves as a networking group. Our everyday lives and interaction with the public can offer just as valuable of an opportunity to network as physically attending a meeting dedicated for networking. A savvy master networker can make an opportunity to connect with other dynamic business people anytime, anywhere. Our lives are so busy that we find ourselves continually on the go. If we stop and look around us, we may very well notice that there are a few like-minded business people around us. Connecting with people outside of a networking environment requires a much more subtle approach. Not only do you have to be subtle, but it is very important to be genuine. If you are out strictly to make a sale then this is the best networking opportunity for you! As a matter of fact, you may find yourself in very awkward situations frequently. I am not saying a sale couldn't happen, because it absolutely could. I am just saying to proceed cautiously and remember, the most authentic connecting approach is always the best approach.

If you are out there to build long lasting, solid business contacts and relationships, then opportunities can present themselves at events such as:

- Holiday parties
- Special events
- Business expos
- Educational workshops and seminars
- Toastmasters
- The Lions Club
- Church functions
- Political functions
- Volunteer events
- Fundraisers
- Sports events
  - ✓ Professional
  - ✓ Recreational
  - ✓ Children's

Each of these environments offers a different experience and valuable opportunity for networking. You can find these events advertised in multiple publications, such as the local newspaper, internet, business journals, business and trade associations and convention center calendars, to mention a few.

Look at your current personal and professional life. The hustle and bustle of life brings us so many different types of networking opportunities. You will quickly see that you won't have to seek out too many other special occasions and events because life continues to present you with so many on-going different ways to meet like-minded professionals.

Take a moment to identify and list opportunities that you currently participate in as well as other's that may be of interest to you in the near future.

Other Networking Opportunities
(This list may continually change)

1. _____

2. _____

3. _____

4. _____

5. _____

Since some of these events are special events and may only come up sporadically, let's focus on the groups and organizations that have a consistent schedule. Just don't discredit the value of the special events and other non-defined networking opportunities. These can potentially attract valuable professionals. It's important to remember that you never know who will turn out to be a great connection.

In order to be the fairest to you, your business and your investment, you are going to want to invest a decent amount of time seeking out the most appropriate groups for you and your business. Identify a few groups that fall into each category within the appropriate targeted area that you identified for your business. This will ensure you are investing your time and not spending your time. Time is a finite resource and you want to ensure you are best utilizing your time at the right meetings, groups and events.

Mystery Shop Before You Join
Now that you have chosen several groups, your homework begins. It is valuable to call and interview the leadership of each of the organizations you listed as being ones you are interested in checking

out. Don't be afraid to ask questions. You are considering making a huge investment with them, not only financially but with your most coveted asset, your time, so be very diligent in your efforts. You will appreciate this step in the future and the organization you are evaluating will respect you for the serious approach you take towards networking.

Some information may already be available to you via the internet or through professional associates, such as:

- Meeting frequency
- Dates and times of meetings
- Duration of meetings
- Meeting locations
- Leadership
- Membership

Meeting logistics is of importance because if it doesn't fit into your routine, both personally and professionally, then you will not attend the meetings. An example to explain this concept is very similar to that gym membership you buy at the beginning of every year and find yourself rarely, or worse yet, never utilizing. Your intentions were good but you fell through on delivery. How effective is that membership really? Be diligent in your efforts. Ask as many questions as you deem appropriate or is necessary to ensure that everything about the meeting's logistics fits into your life's schedule.

The following chart offers some questions that I find valuable to ask when I am considering joining an organization. There are many, many other questions you may think of and many you may not have considered. The list can go on and on but I am certain you will get the gist.

Questions to Consider Before You Join

- ❑ Who attends?
  - ✔ What type of businesses
    - ▸ Small, medium, large corporations
  - ✔ Ask for the who's who list (so to speak)
- ❑ How many members belong to the organization?
- ❑ How many typically attend an event?
  - ✔ If they have multiple events at different times a month
- ❑ What is the structure and the format of their meetings?
- ❑ What is the average duration of the group's members?
  - ✔ Duration may or may not be relevant. If the majority of the membership is relatively new that could either mean the group is in growth mode or there may be a hidden problem. If the majority of the group has been there for a long duration, this could either mean that the group is stable and productive or may be cliquish.
- ❑ How long does leadership hold their positions?
- ❑ Mention your Strategic Referral Partner list, and ask how many members are in those industries and how active they are with the organization?
- ❑ Does the group offer educational opportunities?

- ❑ How many locations do they have?
  - ✔ Is the organization local, regional, national or international organization?
- ❑ Do they have strategic alliances with other networking organizations?
  - ✔ If so, then you may receive membership benefits and discounts
- ❑ Are they For Profit or Non Profit?
- ❑ Do they have/host special events?
- ❑ Do they bring in guest speakers?
- ❑ Do members get speaking spots?
- ❑ Does the organization have a paid or a volunteer staff?
- ❑ How does the group get new members?
- ❑ How do they market the organization and its members?
- ❑ What are the dues for the organization?
  - ✔ Is there a one-time fee or annual membership and how much?
  - ✔ How much are the meeting dues?
- ❑ What types of volunteer opportunities exist for new members?
  - ✔ Servant leadership is very important and will be discussed in the next chapter.

There is no right or wrong answer to any of the questions. You are just information gathering, ensuring that you make a good investment in your business and that you are appropriately investing your time and your advertising dollars.

Now that you have done your due diligence in your interviewing process, which may or may not have enabled you to narrow down your selections, it's time to go out and evaluate these different groups.

You are not attending these meetings as a networker yet, although networking and connecting may organically happen just because you are there. At this point you are just doing research; you are mystery shopping. Realistically speaking, members of organizations typically don't take a visitor seriously until they "put their money where their mouth is" and become a member. Serious members typically view visitors two different ways:

1. As a potential member
2. As a potential customer

Don't take this generalization to mean that nobody is going to connect with you unless you join the group; for the most part this will not be the case.

I want you to approach this as a mystery shopper would, review every detail as an inspection. This is another level of the interviewing process. I want you to be very aware of everything while you are at the meeting.

Go into the "Prospective Meeting Checklist" on pages 98 and 99 with a critical eye. As previously mentioned, assume the perspective of a mystery shopper or a private investigator. This chart includes some things I want you to look for and to be aware of while you are there.

After attending each meeting and having these questions answered, reach out to a few people who you connected with at the meetings and ask them a few questions:

- ❏ How long have **they** been a member?
- ❏ How much business have **they** received from the organization?
  - ✔ From the members?
  - ✔ From referrals from the members?
- ❏ How do **they** like the group?

Once you are armed with information about each of the groups you were interested in, you can make an educated decision about how to move forward and pick the best group or groups for you and your business.

What Should You Choose?

Without knowing specifically what it is you do or how much time and money you have to invest, I can't recommend how many groups you should join. I can however recommend that you diversify. I can also share with you what I do and what I have done in the past. When I first started my business, I joined a category-exclusive, lead and referral generating group. Within a few months of joining this group, I had established a little financial breathing room, so I started diversifying my networking efforts and joined a few other groups and associations that rounded out my needs as a business person, community member, and as a networker. Now I belong to a category exclusive referral generating group, two Chambers of Commerce, three demographic specific groups, and a professional mastermind "by invitation only" group. Last but not least, I am considering joining a couple of professional organizations.

If time and finances allow, I recommend joining a category specific referral group, a local chamber group and a demographic specific group which bests fits you. This allows for a strong and balanced diversification plan. I would also stay in tune with all local expos, special events and other mixers and meetings within the networking area that you had designated.

Prospective Meeting Checklist

- ❏ How did you feel when you walked in?
  - ✓ Nervous, energized, uncomfortable?
- ❏ How were you received/greeted?
  - ✓ Was there a formal greeter?
  - ✓ Did members approach you and make you feel welcomed?
  - ✓ Were you introduced to people who could potentially help your business?
  - ✓ Were people all over you to sell to you?
- ❏ Were you greeted by any of the leadership?
  - ✓ Were you introduced to anyone in leadership?
  - ✓ Did anyone in leadership seek you out to introduce themselves and welcome you?
- ❏ How many members talked to you?
- ❏ What type of venue is the event being held in?
  - ✓ Is the facility dedicated specifically to the event or does it have other activity such as a restaurant?
  - ✓ Is it comfortable?
  - ✓ Is it accessible/easy to find?
  - ✓ How was parking?
  - ✓ Is there room to grow?
- ❏ How was the flow of the meeting?
- ❏ What type of people/businesses attended this meeting?
  - ✓ Is it a category exclusive meeting (closed meeting) or can as many people in the same industry join (open meeting)?
  - ✓ What types of industries/businesses are there?
  - ✓ How is the participants' energy?
  - ✓ Are you familiar with any of the members or businesses?
  - ✓ How many other visitors were there?
    - ▸ This will tell you if the members are actively bringing new prospective members to view the organization.

Prospective Meeting Checklist

❑ Was there a high concentration of a particular industry?

❑ Were there any industries attending that fell into the Strategic Referral Partner classification for your business?

❑ How was the member interaction?
- ✔ Was there a lot of mixing and mingling?
  - ▶ This could be a sign of a productive group
- ✔ Did it seem cliquish?
- ✔ Did you notice little to no movement between the members during the meet and greet process?
- ✔ Did you notice a lot of casual conversation?
  - ▶ This could be a sign of an established social environment

❑ How receptive were people to you?

❑ Were you introduced to anybody?

❑ Did people pay attention to other people?

❑ Was it a selling fest, a social fest or a productive/professional environment?

❑ Were you made to feel as if you belonged?

❑ At the end of the meeting were you approached, received well and invited back or were you just left out on an island?

❑ Did leadership reengage with you?

❑ How did you feel when you left?

❑ After the meeting, whether hours or days, were you contacted by leadership and/or members?
- ✔ If so what was the purpose of their contact?
- ✔ Were they selling you or serving you?

Some organizations have rules about how often you can visit without being a member and others just have different member and non-member entry fees. During your evaluation process, keep this information in the back of your mind. You by no means have to join a group immediately after the first visit. Most organizations typically encourage you to come at least one more time so you can both determine if you are a good fit for each other.

Just remember one important rule: you aren't at the meeting to sell your product or service. You are there seeking initial connections to identify good networking contacts to build your contact sphere. You are there to educate fellow networkers about who you are and what you do as well as being educated by them. Your product or service may generate interest within the attendees, so you may organically develop a buyer/client. It is just not the purpose for your attendance. Remember this; it always helped me.

Communicate To Educate, To Motivate, To Compensate

Master Networker Tip #11
Do your due diligence to find the right networking group(s) for you and your business. If at all possible diversify your approach to networking.

12
Servant Leadership

Finding the right group or groups is only part of the journey. What you do when you become a member will play a large part in the success you have as a member of the organization. Remember, this is a business investment. You are working. You know the old adage, "you get what you give"; well there is definitely some merit to that as it applies to networking. Not just in business given and received, but as it applies to exposure and your ability to differentiate yourself and be memorable. No, this doesn't mean to wear something to stand out, or have a flashy sign, or be the loudest one there, although that would be somewhat entertaining, these are strategies that some people use.

The approach I'm referring to is servant leadership. Put yourself in a position of service. Become a volunteer within the organization. Become an instrumental part of something that you have decided to invest a significant amount of time and energy into to ensure you get the most from your investment.

The Importance of Time Management

Before we get into Servant Leadership and it's importance, I want to bring up what may be going through your mind right now; this networking thing seems extremely cumbersome and time consuming. Honestly, it can be if not managed properly. It can be a huge waste of time, but so can anything in life that isn't done right. Imagine cold calling for hours on end and never getting anywhere, to only find out if you just did this one little thing, your results would have been so much different. Have you ever spent hours prospecting in industrial parks and never getting past a gate keeper because you didn't have the proper skill sets or information? Have you ever wasted countless dollars on publication advertisements or commercials, only to find out that nobody is banging down your door because you ran an ad? When you make a wrong move, it can be a huge waste of your resources, however with a few tweaks and adjustments, the biggest mistakes can turn into your biggest rewards.

Volunteer Positions
& Their Strategies

There are several different opportunities to volunteer within an organization and each position has its own strategies attached to them. Dependent upon your tenure within membership and the position you have chosen or have been chosen to volunteer in will determine the strategic value. Some positions require you to be a little more seasoned member of the group, other positions it doesn't matter how long you have been a member. Ask current leadership what the requirements are to become involved. If you are new, servant leadership is a great opportunity to get involved and get noticed. If you are a seasoned member, servant leadership is a great opportunity to strut your stuff and to give back.

Remember earlier in the book I gave you an exercise to help you understand your personality; especially as it applies to how you "show up" in a sales environment? This is part of the reason why. Knowing how you "show up" will help you figure out which positions are potentially best for you. Regardless of whether you are shy or outgoing, there is a position available for you. If you are shy, being in a position where it is expected of you to approach people, because it is your "job", within the organization will help you ultimately become more comfortable in approaching people you don't know.

Below are a handful of different servant leadership and volunteer opportunities as well as the potential strategic value associated with each. Just remember each organization refers to positions differently, so only use this as a benchmark to identify what is an overall good fit for you.

Visitor Host/Greeters/Chapter Ambassador

This is a natural way to HAVE to meet, greet and introduce yourself to people as it takes the awkwardness out of walking up to people. This is a great position to hold if you are new to networking or shy.

Ambassador

This is typically a position offered in Chambers of Commerce. Ambassadors help welcome new members, follow up on member satisfaction and participate in ribbon cuttings. This position is a good position to hold if your business targets B2B, or if you are shy or have a hard time just walking into businesses and introducing yourself.

Executive Leadership

Most organizations typically have the President, VP, Secretary and Treasurers positions. There is usually a membership term minimum required. You get a lot of exposure in these positions. You are continually in the front of the room which also tends to offer instant credibility for you to new members and visitors. If you have the time these are great positions to hold for continual visibility.

Board of Directors Positions

Usually found within Chambers of Commerce. There is typically a minimum tenure for membership required before you can serve on a Board level position. There is a lot of community work and exposure.

This is only a few of the volunteer opportunities available. Each different type of organization has its own structure and volunteer needs. Regardless of the type of group you join, I strongly recommend getting involved, not only for strategic reasons but also for the obvious. If people don't volunteer the organizations can't properly function. Not to mention the fact that if you directly involve yourself, you are most likely going to attend the majority of the events. Believe it or not, people join groups like this and then never participate. They never show up to meetings and then when it comes time for renewal, they evaluate what they got out of the group. As you would expect, they realize that they didn't get any business out of anybody so they decide not to renew their membership. If you volunteer in a position, you will find your participation will increase and so will your business. Your sphere of influence will naturally follow suit. It is a positive chain of events. I can't recommend this enough. Take baby steps. Don't dive into hours of volunteerism in the beginning. Walk before you run.

Master Networker Tip #12
Put yourself in a volunteer position that challenges your comfort zone. You will find that you will not only grow from this experience but the exposure will help you with your networking efforts.

13

The Connecting Process

To put the connecting process into an analogy that we can all relate too; the connecting process is that first phone call/first couple of "dates" you have after you meet that special someone. You know the one I'm referring to, the one that gave you butterflies in your stomach. Building a relationship with somebody in networking is really no different than the dating process. You are still sharing "intimacies" so to speak but they are professional "intimacies." These are your professional prized possessions, your database, your professional relationships, and most important, your time. The initial connecting process can be difficult, nerve racking or awkward. That is ok, just go with it. I can assure you that for the most part whatever you are experiencing, there is a pretty good chance they are as well.

I do want to clarify though, please do not go into the vacuum vortex of time sucking, by getting caught up in netCHATTING, netSOCIALIZING or netVISITING. Please be very careful and very aware of how much time you spend on personal dialogue. You are both busy and if you are networking properly you are learning about each other's businesses, capabilities and target markets, not about what you did over the weekend or on your vacation or about your kids. A business networking relationship can potentially be very important and key to how successful this type of marketing will be for you. There will be *some* casual conversation, and some personal dialogue, just not a significant amount. Remember what I stated much earlier in the book, people do business with people they like and trust. Because of this, it is important and natural for both of you to connect and share on a personal level. The interpersonal relationship is important. Just do it slowly over time, and make sure that the bulk of the conversation, especially in the beginning, is a balance of business and personal, leaning more on the business emphasis. There needs to be a balance because if the two of you become friends and if the business element is missing, they may never think to refer to you because you are their "friend" and not their Business Referral Partner. They may fail to think of you professionally.

Don't rush out to spend a lot of time with somebody you don't know yet. Don't offer your database openly because remember, your database is your coveted possession; protect it as such. Your reputation is attached to every referral you hand out. Get to know them a little bit first.

Time Allotment

Time is one of your most precious commodities. There never seems to be enough time to do what needs to be done. The time you choose to invest now however, will come back to significantly reward you later. It is important that you be very reasonable, as well as conservative, about the amount of time you are going to budget for networking because if you do not manage it properly it will take a life of its own and get away from you. Budget it conservatively and manage it diligently!

The perfect networking schedule will be completely up to you and how much time you have to dedicate to networking and relationship building. Let's take a look at what is involved in networking. I break it down into three categories:

1. Step 1 - Connecting
2. Step 2 - Relationship establishing
3. Step 3 - Relationship managing

We will break each step down into a multiple step process, so you can be true to yourself in this budgeting process and determine what you can realistically dedicate to networking.

Step 1 – Connecting

Connecting is the beginning stages of networking. As discussed before, connection opportunities and networking opportunities happen in all different types of environments:

- Meetings
- Events
- Mixers
- Socials
- Parties
- Church
- Volunteer events
- Sports
- PTA
- Any other situation which involves people

Our everyday lives bring us many opportunities to connect with people and because of this you want to ensure that you are always on. You never know who you are going to bump into. Whether it is a social event or a professional meeting environment, always bring your "A" game.

For the purpose of putting together a plan we will approach this based on a meeting / event. However, do not negate the importance of the other connecting and networking opportunities as we will discuss those strategies a little later.

1. Attending a networking meeting / Event
   a. Commute time   = _____ minutes
   b. Arrive Early   =   30 minutes
   c. Event   = _____ minutes
   d. After event connecting =   30 minutes
   e. Commute time   = _____ minutes

You will find in most cases, going to a networking meeting or an event to meet people will easily be an average investment of 3 - 3 ½ hours.

This is a significant amount of time and you haven't even started truly networking yet. You have only started netCONNECTING. I hope by looking at the required time allotment that you have a better understanding of how important it is now to have a networking plan, and a more clear understanding of:

- What meeting you are going to attend
- Why you are going to a networking meeting
- Who you want to meet while you are at the meeting
- What you are going to say while you are there
- What you are going to do when you leave

Step 1a – After Meeting Organization

Before we go any further, I need you to do me a favor. I need you to throw a sharpie and rubber bands into a box of sandwich baggies and take them out to your car and put them in the back seat. You will understand why soon.

You went to a networking meeting, good for you, now what? You haven't really even started truly networking yet. What you do now is where the real work begins, where the rubber meets the road so to speak. What you do after you leave the meeting from this point on determines your success in networking and building relationships.

As I stated earlier, networking and netconnecting really are just like dating, think about it. You go out with some friends; you meet somebody that you have a good feeling about, then what do you do? Get married the next day? NO! You call them, you court each other. Professional networking and relationship building is no different. This is where the courting begins.

In the past, when I got back to my office after leaving a meeting, I sent an email to each person I talked to thanking them for their time. I would mention something briefly that we discussed so that they would remember me and I let them know one of two things:

1. I look forward to getting to know more about them and that I would see them at the next event.

-OR-

2. I will call them within the next couple days to schedule some time to meet with them.

That follow through used to work great but it seems that recently people are so inundated with emails and technology that email is more of a delayed burden than it is a classy touch. In some cases it may still be appreciated. I personally have gotten away from doing that because of how over loaded people are with email. I play it by ear now, sometimes I will:

- Send an email
- Send a card
- Make a follow up call within the period of time I committed
- Let them know when I exited our conversation that I look forward to seeing them at the next meeting

It really just depends on the situation, so that is why I play it by ear.

It is still very important that you follow through with your commitments, your word, and your promises. You must maintain your integrity and display the highest levels of professionalism. If you say you are going to call them by a certain date and time, then make sure that you do. If you schedule an appointment with them, then show up. Always ensure that you respect their time as well as yours. There is nothing worse than making the impression that you are flakey through unprofessional actions.

Don't be one of those networkers who are all hyped up and ends up over-committing and under-delivering. You know them: I love you, you love me, let's get together and have coffee, and then you never hear from them ever again until the next time you see them and then it's the same song and dance. Be grateful that you don't hear from them again. They are time and energy vacuums. I like to call them networking vampires, because they suck you dry. Do not be one of these black holes. You want and need to offer value. The formula is easy: do what you say and say what you do, and be authentic, congruent and transparent while you do "it".

A sure-fire way to lose credibility instantly is to not call, show up or do whatever it is you committed to do.

This is what I do when I walk out of a networking event.

- After I leave a meeting, I get into my car and empty out my pockets or planner (if I don't have pockets) and gather up all the cards I have.
  - ✔ I have a sorting mechanism that I use so I am careful not to mix up the cards
    - ▸ Business cards from my **RIGHT** side are people that I see a potential Strategic Referral Partner relationship with in the future
    - ▸ Business cards from my **LEFT** are people that I will get to know in the future and will definitely see around at other meetings. They are still possible referral sources but I don't think they fit into the definition of potential Strategic Referral Partner
- I make notes, on a post it, on each business card that is in my right pocket and paper clip each one to its respective business card
- Remember the box of sandwich bags? Grab them out of the back seat and sift and sort
  - ✔ Write on the bag with the sharpie
  - ✔ Event name
  - ✔ Date
  - ✔ Time
  - ✔ Location
- I put the business cards I gathered in the bag
  - ✔ My **RIGHT** cards I rubber band them together and put them in the bag

- ✓ My **LEFT** cards I put them in the bag loosely
  - ▸ I put the baggie on the seat of my car or in my planner and go on with the rest of my day

For me, the baggie trick is the only thing that keeps me sane. I network an insane amount of time and used to have business cards all over the place. Within 24 hours, I would forget who was who, and whom I met where. Sometimes I only network once a day but there are times when I will go to two or three events in a day and in order to keep everything straight and organized (and to avoid those unwanted arguments in the house about my business card messes), it was just neater and more organized to implement this method.

After a productive day of working and networking, I always make sure I have time in my day to work on my CRM (Customer Relationship Management Program). I update my CRM and schedule my follow-up calls for the next day.

Step 2 – Establishing the Relationship

During the course of a meeting, you exchanged casual conversation, identified what they did, what company they worked for or owned, how long they have been there and potentially what an ideal client is for them. Pretty much all the basic stuff. Now you want to get to know them a little more. I will fall back on what I have said several times already, your time is your most valuable and prized asset, so be very conscientious who you spend or invest your time with accordingly.

There are a few different ways you can get to know them a little bit better. You can call them and talk a little on the phone to see how much you both can help each other's businesses, or you can meet with them over coffee or at one or the other's office so you can really see what each other does. Sometimes I will talk with somebody over the phone and then meet with them and sometimes I will meet with them face to face for a little one-to-one face time. It really just depends on multiple factors:

- Their schedule
- My schedule
- What they do
- If our target markets complement each other

I always try to ensure we both get the biggest bang for our buck. There isn't enough time in the day to meet with that many people, network, build relationships, service customers and oh yeah, run my business. So I ensure that when I meet with someone that the meeting is of value for both of us.

Step 2a - The Follow-Up Call

This is where the dance begins, or to play with the analogy I have been continually referencing, this is where the courtship begins.

How will this person/business fit into your professional life? Only time will tell; however, with a little due diligence, effort and commitment, the two of you can realize pretty quickly how the puzzle pieces are going to fit together. It is very important to have time blocked out for this call because you don't want to be distracted by other things; multi-tasking is not a good idea here. You want and need to be fully present, so don't do this while you are driving or in front of your computer answering emails. Honor the time you blocked out for this: you will thank yourself later.

When you connected at the event, something triggered you to put their business card into your follow-up pocket. If you worked the event properly, you only had a chance to spend less than five minutes with them, so this is where you get to spend a little bit more time to see how much the two of you can help each other.

The last thing you want to do is start this relationship off on the wrong foot. You will want to ensure that your new found professional acquaintance has time to talk with you. When they answer the phone, you aren't sure what is going on at that moment for them, so it is always best to ask if this is a good time for them to talk. Don't just dive into a conversation making it awkward for them to have to pipe up and ask if they can call you back. I am sure you are professional and aware of this; I just believe it is very important and shouldn't go without saying.

Now that you have your new-found business acquaintance on the phone, and you have identified that this is good time for them to talk, you essentially want to pick up where you left off at the meeting. After a comfortable couple minutes of casual conversation, you want to get down to business, remembering you are both busy professionals. There is a list of questions I use that I have found over the years that has best worked for me in growing my relationships, Strategic Referral Partnerships and my business. I don't use all of them in every conversation. I keep the conversation natural; remember it is about building a relationship, so it requires authenticity and congruency. In order for the relationship to be successful, you have to be comfortable so everything has to flow naturally. I will share with you my dialogue and questions:

*I let them know at the beginning of my conversation that I realized after meeting them; I really wanted to get to know more about them and their business. That based off our brief conversation I realized there was a possibility we had a potential to be able to help **each other grow our businesses.** Then I would ask them if they were interested in exploring the opportunity?*

Their answer would depend on what I would say next. You see, if their answer was "no, not really" or something like that, or if they didn't sound optimistic or enthusiastic, then we both saved a lot of time by not meeting for coffee or lunch. We shared only about five minutes of pleasant conversation, I had the opportunity to increase my knowledge of another business and person and I gracefully end the conversation with something like…" It was really great talking with you and having the opportunity to get to know you a little better. I look forward to getting to know you more in the future and seeing you at the next meeting."

I don't get defensive; I don't get my feelings hurt. I am very grateful that we established the fact that there wasn't an interest up front instead of using valuable time driving to a destination to have a face-to-face meeting only to find out the same information. There could be several reasons why this person isn't interested and I don't let myself worry about those reasons. Just because there isn't an interest now doesn't mean there might not be one in the future. So I made a new business acquaintance, nothing wrong with that at all.

After I hang up the phone I update my CRM. I change their category from **Potential Strategic Referral Partner** to whatever industry they are in, and I move on to my next call. Now do you see why you need to be fully present during this phone call? I can't emphasize enough the importance of being tuned in to them and giving them your undivided attention.

Now if they say they are interested in pursuing the possibility of helping each other grow our businesses, this is where I get excited and the fun begins.

I ask them if they have some time to talk now and if I could ask them a few questions which should take less than 10 minutes. I tell them that I truly take my responsibility as a networking partner very seriously and I need to understand a little more about their business so that we can be of value to each other.

I created a form with these questions on it so I can write their answers down. This enables me to listen intently so I don't miss anything and then I can go back later to update my CRM.

Potential Strategic Referral Partner Telephone Questions

1. Tell me a little bit more about your business?
   There is only so much we could learn in the few minutes we had at the meeting, so I want to get a better understanding.

2. **What are your responsibilities for the business?**

I want to know if they are an owner, partner or an employee. I want to know if they are on the front lines, involved in the day-to-day, and a decision maker.

3. **Who is your target market?**

I want to know if I have a relationship with somebody who I may be able to immediately refer if I believe my credibility would be protected, and I need this information moving forward if we are a good fit to be Strategic Referral Partners.

4. **What specific industries do you best serve?**

I ask this for the same reason I ask the question regarding target market.

5. **Who are your major competitors?**

I ask this question for a few reasons. First of all, do I know any of them? Second, does anybody I know utilize their competitors and lastly, this is useful information moving forward if we become Strategic Referral Partners because I know what to listen for when I talk with other people.

6. **What industries are good referral sources for you?**

I am asking this for the same reasons I asked the last few questions.

7. **How do you grow your business?**

This question is a little self serving. I need to know, if they market, if they network, are they a go getter, are they an action maker, or do they sit around and wait for things to happen.

At this point you have a good amount of information about them to determine whether or not you can offer value to them and if they can offer value to you. During this questioning and interaction, they may or may not ask the same questions of you. It is helpful if they do though because this gives them an opportunity to get to know a little bit more about you as well. It isn't necessary at this point, however be careful that this doesn't become a one sided relationship.

If you do decide there is potential for this relationship to become a strong reciprocal referral relationship and you chose to move on to the next step of getting to know each other, then you will have the opportunity at that time to establish some expectations. Remember, you are out there connecting and networking to add value to people, businesses and ultimately your business. You want to add value not only to the people you are meeting, but to the people in your life both personally and professionally.

You are working to create the image of a one-stop referral shop. When people start thinking of you to provide a connection/a referral when they have a need, want or desire, it is because they know you know the best of the best. This is when you know you are on the right path to success. Think about it, when you have people calling you for anything they need, even if it isn't something you offer, you are in a very powerful position. That means you have people thinking of you! Do you realize how much money the "Big Boys" pay daily in advertising, just to get the average consumer to think about them? Now you have put yourself in a position where people are calling you. **Now that is leverage!**

Step 3 – Relationship Management

Both of you have done a lot of due diligence by this point. You have both realized that there is a lot of validity in investing time with each other and in moving forward to the next level of your referral partnership. By continuing to build this partnership, you have both realized that there is a level of financial reward and reciprocation by helping each other and partnering with each other. So like any other successful relationship in life, this requires effort on both your parts. You really want to invest yourself fully in this process because this truly is the pot of gold at the end of the rainbow. This will require some work; hence the word, netWORKING. That is OK. Time invested properly will be rewarded significantly.

Step 3a – The Follow Up Meeting(s)

Follow up meetings can and will come in all shapes and sizes, and their frequency and duration will vary, not only from meeting to meeting, but also from person to person. Each relationship is significantly different and has to be treated as such. Some meetings will be less intense; some will be over the phone, some will be quick and some will be long. No matter what the dynamics of the meetings are, one thing for certain is that you are in a building mode; this is a great place to be. This is exciting. Just look at how many opportunities the two of you are going to open and create for each other.

Initially, you are going to want to be somewhat prepared for these meetings. I use the term "somewhat" loosely. What I mean by this is, have a purpose, bring marketing collateral and information if you have any so that you can review it with them as well as give it to them to keep and share. Bring a list of questions you want to have a better understanding of as well as bullet points that you don't want to forget to share about yourself. Bring a notepad and pen; don't be afraid to take notes. I used the term "somewhat" specifically because, as I have stated a few times, relationships are about authenticity, congruency, transparency and presence. If you are going through a check list or a script and you are not comfortable and being yourself, then you are doing this relationship building process a huge injustice.

It is you that they want/need to get to know. So let the process happen naturally.

Master Networker Tip #13

1. Be Present
2. Be Authentic
3. Be Congruent
4. Be Transparent
5. Genuinely Care About Them
6. Treat Them Like A Person
   and Not Like A $

   BE YOURSELF!

14
Networking Burnout?

I am often asked if it's possible to get burned out from networking. The answer is yes and no. I had a mentor share valuable words with me that I believe fit this topic, "what we feed grows and what we starve dies." The harder we work, the more necessary it is for us to refuel and recharge. Burnout happens, it is natural for those of us who give it our all and go full throttle in everything we do. So that being said, I don't believe a Master Networker gets burned out from networking, I believe they just get burned out and need to respect themselves and recharge.

I do believe that it is possible for a Networker to get burned out on a particular group or organization for a multitude of reasons.

Ended Up in the Wrong Environment
Do your due diligence. It is vitally important to join groups that can best serve you and that you can best serve. Don't be a serial joiner and just join any group or organization because someone told you that you had to network in order to grow your business.

Group/Organization Dynamics Changed
Groups and Organizations go through different cycles and because of this the group may be stagnant. If that is the case, instead of immediately abandoning ship, step up, show them what you are made out of, and take action in a non leadership role. Bring guests, make connections become even more valuable then what you already are. If the group is at all revivable your leadership efforts will recharge enough people to take the group off of life support.

You Aren't Receiving Any Referrals or Business

It is hard to stay motivated when you aren't seeing any results. I am a firm believer that before we ever look externally we want to look internally.

What do I mean by this?

Internal Reflection

- How effective are your commercials?
- Are you conducting Referral Partner Meetings (RPMs) and how effective are they?
- Are you actively making connections for other people?
- Are you continually offering quality referrals?
- Do you have an understanding of the tipping point for referability of your industry? Depending on the sensitivity and nature of your product or service, will depend on how much of an investment in time you will need to make before you see a return. Understanding this is very key to not setting yourself up to fail.
- What food choices are you making and are you exercising? Yes, I went there. It is very hard to eat healthy in these environments. Because of this, you want to take care of the machine, your body that takes care of you and your business. If you are out networking as much as I am, a couple times a day several days a week, your "diet" may not be the best. No matter how hard I try it is very difficult to stay within a healthy nutritional balance. The portions are usually larger than they should be, restaurants may cook in unhealthy butters or oils. The calories for one meal alone may exceed your Recommended Daily Allowance (RDA). Some valuable tips to keep in mind while you are out there are:
- Eat ½ your plate and take the other ½ home.
- Make sensible meal selections, no matter how tempting those double cheeseburgers and fries are.
- Keep a consistent exercise routine.

External Reflection
- Has the group's dynamics significantly changed since I became a member? If I am B2B focused has the group added so many B2C members that the focus has shifted to B2C or vice versa.
- Did the group stop growing? Did members stop bringing guests? Did new members stop joining?
- What is the dynamic of the leadership team?
- Is the venue a hindrance and effecting the groups dynamics?
- Is the affordability of the organization and/or the meeting dues effecting membership drive?
- What is the membership's support and participation with each other?
- What is the success level of the members? Are the members growing and thriving entrepreneurs or are they desperate entremanuers?

When you have done all you can do and no matter what a group isn't reviving, move on. Your vitality is that much more important. Do this with finesse, with the utmost levels of professionalism. Do not exit burning bridges. Remember you are there to build relationships and just because it didn't work out in that environment, you never know when you will run into some of these fellow networkers again. I do suggest this very rarely, and only when it is essentially and vitally necessary. One of the biggest mistakes a networker makes is thinking that if they leave a Group or an Organization, that the members there will still use them and refer to them. This is rarely the case. For the most part, the old adage, "out of sight out of mind" truly applies once you chose not to continue your membership. So before making this decision, really dig deep and evaluate your options.

There are other dynamics to consider if you are starting to feel a little burned out.

- Take a look at your networking routine. Mix it up a little. Visit meetings and events you have never been to.

- If you go to meetings or events alone, take a friend. If you continual take people with you to meetings and events, go alone.
- Network at different times of the day. Go to an evening event instead of a morning event.
- Get even more creative collaborating with your Referral Partners and your Strategic Referral Partners.

No matter what, keep plugging away. WOMM and Referral Marketing are strong value based solutions for you and your company. Take care of you so you can take care of your business. The minor steps and actions you take today will grow into huge results tomorrow.

Master Networker Tip #14
Before blaming others,
always look within.
It is not necessarily
what we are seeing and more likely
how we are seeing it.

15

The Importance of a Networking Plan

Do you know people spend more time planning their vacations then they do planning their business, marketing and networking strategies? I don't know if that is scary or sad. Running a business is tough; trust me I know. I completely understand that we run lean and mean. However, if we take the time now to develop a plan, put it in place, and create a system, everything will get easier with time. We basically have two options:

Option 1- Plan
Be prepared and get a decent ROI

Option 2 - Ready – Shoot – Aim
This seems to be the more typical approach. Just showing up with no understanding of what you want to accomplish or who you want to meet. This is not a productive approach at all, but the one most frequently used.

I am not going to pull wool over your eyes. This isn't going to be easy, and this is going to take a lot of work and dedication. But the payoff is huge; it works if you work it. There is a reason why this old adage exists: "if you fail to plan then you plan to fail." There is so much truth wrapped up in that one statement. OK, I am off my soap box for now, so let's get down to business.

Throughout this entire book, you have been developing the necessary stages to prepare yourself for developing your networking plan. We just have to put it together, tune it up and have it all flow and make sense.

Time Allocation

As previously stated, time is one of your most valuable assets. Yes, I am aware that I say that a lot. Reality is that time is a finite resource and needs to be respected. It is so important to invest it properly to ensure that you get the biggest bang for your buck.

1. How much time do you have on a monthly basis to invest in networking?
2. How much of this time will you allocate to networking events/meetings?
3. How much time are you projecting to invest in face-to-face meetings?
4. How much of this time are you allocating to Strategic Referral Partners?
5. Total projected allocated time?

Now that you have identified how much time you have to invest, where and with whom are you going to invest your time?

Groups & Organizations

Ensuring that you belong to the right group(s) and organization(s) is imperative to your success in networking. If you did your homework in Chapter 11, this exercise will be easy for you to quickly complete.

1. How many groups does it make sense for you to join right now based on your finances and available time?
2. Which group(s) best resonate with you and your business needs?
3. If you are considering joining more than one group, what is the mix you are considering? (Lead & Referral Group, Chamber of Commerce, Community and Demographic Specific Group, Non Profit Organization)
4. What special events/expos come to your area that could potentially be a good networking opportunity for you that is of interest to you?

5. What group(s) are you going to join?
6. What is the meeting(s) frequency and what day(s) do they meet?

You can stay in limbo trying to pick a group(s) for an extended period of time. This does nothing but cause you unnecessary confusion and delays your ability to get down to business. So I am going to hold a flame under you and have you make a decision based on your previous homework. Do your due diligence, make your decision, make the investment and become a member of an organization. A group and the members within a group really don't take you seriously until you put your money where your mouth is.

Show Up
Showing up means so many things:

- Your branding and appearance
- Your mood
- Your ability to be in the present moment
- Physically working the room at a meeting/event

All of which we will address now.

Branding
How do you want to be viewed/known uniform, suit, business casual, informal or very casual? I ask this because this is how you are going to brand yourself for the most part. I am a pretty laid back business casual to casual person. If I could wear jeans all the time I would. I really don't enjoy wearing suits and dressing professionally, however I recognize that there are times when I need to. No matter what, I always stay true to myself so that I remain authentic at all times. If you wear a uniform to perform your work, there really isn't anything wrong with wearing it to the meetings. It all depends on you and how you want to be viewed.

Show Up Prepared

Have you ever shown up to a meeting without business cards? Well, don't! It is hard for you to connect with people without a way to deliver your contact information. There is one exception to this rule, and that is if you are a very seasoned networker and you are confident in your ability to finesse and not offend. Then by not handing out a business card, and controlling the flow and management of the initial engagement and relationship is a brilliant strategy. I will repeat, YOU MUST BE A SEASONED NETWORKER to pull this off.

Other notable areas to ensure you are prepared are:

- Clear understanding of who you want to meet
- Have any pertinent marketing material
- Commercial strategy prepared

Be Present

When you approach somebody, don't drift off while they are talking to you. You need to hear and know what they are saying. Don't be looking around the room for the next person you want to meet. Devote the time to them, listen to them and be present while you are with them.

Leave your day at the door before you walk into the meeting. No matter what your day was like before you went to the meeting, DO NOT bring it into the meeting with you. I personally get to a meeting a little earlier and sit in my car and do a quick meditation and grounding exercise. I have found that this helps me be fully present and gives me the energy and ability to "play full out."

Work

- How are you going to add value to an organization?
  - ✔ What position are you choosing to volunteer for?
- How are you going to work the room?

- Who are you going to meet? This is a huge part of "showing up." It really does you no good if you go to an event and don't meet new people.
- Who is in the room?
- Who can offer value to your business and whose business can you offer value to? You don't know unless you meet NEW people! Keyword there is NEW.
  - ✓ Make a point to connect with:
    - ▸ Speakers
    - ▸ Leadership
    - ▸ Members of Interest

Follow Up

Going to events and meetings and joining groups is part of the formula. If you don't follow up with people you meet or reach out to get to know people better you won't get too much out of networking. After you schedule meetings in your calendar, immediately block out follow up time and computer time.

I typically schedule out my networking calendar two to three weeks in advance. I then block out computer time daily to organize myself, allowing time for business card scanning and database (CRM) updating. I ensure that I do this the same day for each event as that allows me to recall specific things I need to remember as well as conversations I may have had that I can notate. I also block out time to make phone calls to follow up with people I have met if there was a mutual interest. I typically schedule this within a couple days of the meetings I attend. I usually try to ensure I do this the very next day. It's not good to let too much time go by before you reestablish contact because people are busy. *I know this is hard to believe, but yes, they can actually forget about you.* Just make sure you have the time blocked out to make these calls and don't put it off for something that may seem more important. If you are including networking in your marketing and advertising plan, then the follow up portion of networking is **VERY IMPORTANT!**

Relationship Management

One of the main reasons I plan my calendar in advance is so that I can allocate time to build and manage relationships. Building and developing relationships is the key to success in networking. You want to treat this time as you would time you spend with a valued customer, prospect, board meeting or a sales meeting. The time spent developing and managing these relationships is just as important as any of the above-mentioned meetings. You are building a relationship with an advocate. You are adding a valued resource to your database. This is a potential "go to" person when somebody who you know has a need for their product or service and vice versa.

Summing It Up

Remember that aside from all this networking, you still have a business to run. That is why identifying your commitment level, your needs, wants and purpose for networking and the time you have available is important. Because realistically speaking, if it becomes a hindrance and if you view it as an unproductive aspect of doing business, you will not follow through. I am here to tell you again that if you do it right, it will be a huge part of your business.

Master Networker Tip #15
Follow through with developing your plan and your plan will follow through with developing your business.

16
Journey to Becoming a Master Networker

Becoming a Master Networker doesn't happen overnight. It is an ongoing process, and it a journey, not a destination. Like anything in life, to become a Master, you have to work at it. As a matter of fact, you have to work at it a lot. That is okay though because with work comes reward. And this journey will prove to be very rewarding. Take it slow; don't try to conquer the world of networking overnight; relationships take time to cultivate. Be true to yourself and the process. Be diligent and be of value. Ensure that you are doing this for the right reasons; people will see right through you otherwise. Don't pretend to be in it to serve and add value yet the whole time you are keeping your product or service hidden behind your back just waiting for the right moment to spring it on them to "close the deal."

Throughout this entire book, I have given you tools that, if applied, will help you achieve success in networking. Remember why "YOU" have chosen to utilize networking as part of your marketing and advertising plan. Everybody's reasons are different, and although there are no right or wrong reasons, your reasons will greatly impact the level of success you get from networking.

For me, I am very clear as to why I have incorporated networking into my marketing plan.

- Being a professional conduit of quality products, services and solutions adds extreme value to my relationships:
  - ✓ Family
  - ✓ Friends
  - ✓ Clients
  - ✓ Prospects
  - ✓ Fellow Networkers
- The level of representation that Word of Mouth marketing offers is far more economical than hiring multiple sales people
- Networking offers a focused target marketing plan, as opposed to the "Ready-Shoot-Aim" approach
- Developing strong professional relationships allows me to surround myself with like-minded professionals. This forces me to "step up" my performance
- My professional relationships and knowledge of who is who in a marketplace make me the first person people in my database think of when they need something. When there is a need, no matter what it is, I get a call. "Hey do you know anybody who...???" I get to help people and in return I get helped

I have a quick short story for you. As I have shared with you, I belong to many networking organizations and serve in multiple levels of leadership in them all. I practice what I preach, which is how I know it works. In one of the organizations I belong to, I serve is as an ambassador. As part of this responsibility, I make follow up calls with members throughout the term of their membership. This particular call was in the last quarter of a member's membership.

I was given a list of questions which I reviewed with her and I documented her answers and then returned it back to the organization for their records.

Here is how the call went:

Me – *Hi, my name is Stacey O'Byrne. I am an ambassador for "XYZ Chamber of Commerce" that you are also a member of. I am calling on behalf of the organization to follow up on your satisfaction with your* *membership and have a few questions to ask you. This will take about five minutes, is now a good time?*

Member – *Yeah sure I guess.*

Me – *Great, thank you. Before we get started though, I am looking at your website and have a few questions for you. I sit on a board of directors for a non-profit and your product looks like an amazing way to raise funds. I have never seen you at any of the Chamber's meetings or events. I would love to get some more info on your business. The non-profit that I sit on the board of has a board meeting in approximately four weeks and I would like to show your company information to the directors to see if we can incorporate your products into a new fund raising campaign this year.*

Member – *That's exactly the kind of stuff I want to get my company involved in, I am not a onesy – twosey manufacturer. This is the perfect opportunity for my business.*

Me – *Great. At our next board meeting I will show them your website, and will let you know how it goes.*

Member – *That's perfect. I have really been trying to get into the non-profit arena for a while. So what questions did you have for me?*

Me – Since joining, has the Chamber met all of your expectations?

Member – *I haven't really had any expectations, so yes, I guess.*

Me – Have you had the opportunity to attend any of the Chamber's meetings or events?

Member – *No, not really. Well a couple, but networking really doesn't work for me or my business. I went to a couple meetings but stopped going after that. It's just not worth the $300 or $400 I spent for my membership.*

Me – *Oh, I'm sorry to hear that. I am a little confused though. I don't mean for this to be awkward in any way, but you do realize that what I just offered to you with the non-profit and opening that door up for you is greatly due to the fact that you belonged to this Chamber. I would have never found you otherwise. Honestly, if you had come to the meetings, we would have met much sooner, and I could have potentially opened this door up for you over a year ago. And think about it, how many more people like me are out there, with a relationship that could potentially open multiple more doors for you and your company?*

Member – *I did go, I tried it. I went to two or three meetings over the past nine months and never got anything.*

Me – *I am sorry to hear that. That isn't quite networking, but I understand. I just have a few more questions for you. Have you participated in the organization's weekly group meetings?*

Member – *No, not really. After I went to a couple events, I just realized it was a waste of my time. So I never went to the weekly group meetings.*

Me – *Are you part of any committees?*

Member – *No, didn't see value in it.*

Me – *Are you aware of the tools and free advertising the organization's website offers?*

Member – *Yes, just never took advantage of it.*

Me – *How can we better serve you and your needs?*

Member – *You can't really, I am not going to renew. This networking thing really doesn't work for me.*

Me – *Well, that is it for the questions. I really appreciate your time. I wish I could help you see the value of being an active member.*

Member – *Thanks so much, let me know how it goes with the board meeting. That is a huge organization and I would love to get my business into their fund raising campaign.*

Where do I start? Am I the only one that sees something wrong with that whole conversation? I have to be honest with you, during the last five minutes of that conversation, I felt like I was having an out of body experience. It isn't my place to educate her on behalf of the organization. It is only my place to gain information and pass it along. I didn't want to make her feel uncomfortable by saying, "No duh, it's not working. It only works if you work it. You get out of something exactly what you put into it!" It is very hard for me to not jump up on that soap box, but it wasn't appropriate. So I fought the urge, no matter how hard it was to resist. I was and still am speechless. I hope you see something wrong with what I just shared with you. It truly is one of the reasons I wrote this book.

There are just a few more helpful tips, secrets and key reminders that I want to plant in your mind. These are very important during your journey to becoming a master networker and ensuring your efforts will create productive networking.

The Be, Do, Have of Networking

Be Prepared
Have your introduction and commercials prepared in your head so you aren't tongue-tied when you meet someone new.

Be Informed
Read the paper, either off-line or on-line, so you know what's going on in the community and the world. Be sure you are versed on current events.

Be Authentic
Be sure that you are truly present and partake in the conversation. DO NOT make the mistake of following the advice of 'small talk'

experts who say, "Just ask people questions because people love to talk about themselves." If all you do is ask questions, you offer nothing to the conversation. People will feel uneasy around you because you really aren't being present in the relationship building process.

Be Personable
Treat people as people, not as prospects.

Be Transparent
Remember, people do business with people they like and trust. The more transparent you are the easier you are to like and trust.

Be Professional
First impressions are lasting impressions; this is unfortunate but true. Ensure you are representing yourself exactly how you want to be perceived while staying true to yourself.

Be Attentive/Present
LISTEN to what people say instead of planning your next line or looking for the perfect opportunity to shove your product or service down their throat. They are telling you what they want to talk about and you can take a hint and build meaningful conversation that has joint participation.

Be Realistic
Start small; establish a connection and you will organically build to the bigger topics. Don't try to get married on the first date, so to speak.

Be Real
Remember; Facts Tell – Stories Sell. Share stories that relate to the interests of others because people connect with our stories, not facts, features, benefits or sales pitches.

Be Respectful

When you meet somebody for the first time, don't assume that they want you to contact them, let alone put them on your newsletter list. Ask permission, ask them if they mind if you reach out to them and contact them. By all means, observe netETIQUETTE at all times. DO NOT SPAM people. Allow them to opt-in to your newsletter.

Remember...

The majority of the people you will meet are nice. They are seeking the same things you are; true relationships which are mutually beneficial.

The more time you spend developing mutually beneficial relationships and staying true to your networking plan, the more valuable of a Master Networker you will become. This journey is very rewarding both socially and financially. Be true to your plan and your plan will be true to you.

Throughout your journey to becoming a Master Networker please feel free to stop by our website www.themasternetworker.com to check out our latest tools and resources and to find out information on upcoming workshops which will be of benefit to you now and in your future success. Just remember, networking is not something you can do alone. So those are the "Secrets to Becoming a Master Networker." We are here to help you become the successful Master Networker you want to be. I look forward to hearing from you and seeing you out there.

Master Networker Tip #16

Work your plan and your plan will work.
Be real; be true to you and your business
and most of all be true to your
Referral Partners and offer meaningful value.

Made in the USA
Charleston, SC
04 February 2014